L‘

TRAV.

21/02

THE
INDOMITABLE
BEATIE

THE INDOMITABLE BEATIE

CHARLES HOARE, C.B. FRY and the CAPTAIN'S LADY

RONALD MORRIS

SUTTON PUBLISHING

First published in the United Kingdom in 1985 by
Chatto & Windus as *The Captain's Lady*.
First published in this revised and expanded edition in 2004 by
Sutton Publishing Limited · Phoenix Mill
Thrupp · Stroud · Gloucestershire · GL5 2BU

British Library Cataloguing in Publication Data
A catalogue record for this book is available from the British Library.

ISBN 0-7509-3710-6

Typeset in 11/14.5pt Sabon.
Typesetting and origination by
Sutton Publishing Limited.
Printed and bound in England by
J.H. Haynes & Co. Ltd, Sparkford.

To Emily and Oliver

'And let me speak to th' yet unknowing world
How these things came about.'

Hamlet, Act V. Scene II

Contents

List of Plates

Preface

In the shadow of a remarkable man it is just possible there might be an even more remarkable woman. This was certainly the case with C.B. Fry who died in 1956 at eighty-four. The woman was his wife, Beatrice Holme Fry. She did not seem to begrudge her husband his pre-eminence, relieved, perhaps, that it took the spotlight off herself and her dark beginnings. As a young woman and a celebrated beauty, her affair with one of the richest men in England, the heir to a banking fortune and a married man, had scandalised the noble circles in which they moved, and provided compulsive reading in the Press of the day.

As a boy of fifteen, I encountered Mrs Fry in the last seven months of her life when I joined the *Mercury*, the training ship for boys that she ran on the Hamble in southern England, and experienced first hand her powerful and sometimes terrifying presence. The impression she made was such that I determined to discover the circumstances that brought this personality into being. There can be few instances – if any – of a woman at that time proving so successful in adjunct to what was probably regarded as the most manly of occupations, beginning at a time when the rules of society, and especially the class into which she was born, debarred most women from roles that were other than menial, domestic or decorative. In a more generous time, and given the freedom and also the education that women were denied, she could have led nations.

In her everyday dealings with people she seemed devoid of the fear that she generated in all but a very few, most of them men of immense power, authority and wealth. But every day she walked in fear of her past being exposed so that even the few might desert her. Wealth she had in abundance, so she would never be without material comforts. The real loss would be of a way of life that gave her deep satisfaction even though it weighed heavily on those who shared the same roof. Among the crushed were three daughters. One was in her thirties, one twenty-five, before they could escape. The third, an almost spectral figure, had to wait for her mother's death before she too could get away.

C.B. Fry was at the height of his powers when he married Beatrice in 1888, the most admired and adulated figure in British public life, who came to be described as perhaps the most variously gifted Englishman of any age.[1] For J.B. Priestley a list of men who were most characteristically English had to include Fry, together with Ralegh, Pepys, Samuel Johnson, Charles Lamb, Michael Faraday and Richard Burton the explorer; he wrote of his special fondness for Fry, who appeared to him as a Renaissance man, a legendary figure even in his own lifetime.[2]

Priestly never met Fry, but his judgement was unerring insofar as his admiration was for the man as a natural all-rounder. He had only to take up a game to master it and he was the greatest all-round sportsman of his era, perhaps of all time. Americans heard of him in 1891 when, aged nineteen, he equalled the world long jump record set by C.S. Reber at Detroit the same year. The record stood for twenty years. He was in addition a brilliant scholar, Oxford graduate, writer, and friend and confidant of world figures, but in spite of all his gifts his wife towered over him at least in their domestic realm. She may prove to be the last great unsung character of her generation – and this is her story.

Acknowledgements

A work of this nature involves many people whose contributions one is bound and happy to acknowledge. However, in the years since I began my research, a number of those who helped me have died. I list them, therefore, without distinction.

I am grateful to Mr M. Hoare, Miss K. Potter and the committee of the *Mercury* Old Boys' Association for access to their collections of papers and pictures. These illuminate a small but vital aspect of British maritime history.

I spent a memorable afternoon with Stephen, son of the late C.B. Fry, and his wife Yvonne, who encouraged me in my research. Joan Begbie and Mrs Adria Hoare, daughter-in-law of Charles Hoare, contributed enormously to my research with material and memories too numerous to list. Joan Begbie was particularly informative because she was a frequent visitor to Hall Place, the home of Charles Hoare in the decade preceding his death, and to the *Mercury* as the guest of Captain and Mrs Fry thereafter. For a short spell she taught there.

Dick Robinson grew up in the shadow of the *Mercury*. He helped me with information and with advice, as also did Mr and Mrs Tremlett of Kenn in Devon, whose home was that of Margaret Baring Short when she married Charles Hoare in 1867. They permitted my brother Norman to photograph family portraits, and their reproduction in my book.

The archivists, librarians and historians who helped are: Sir Robin Mackworth-Young KCVO, FSA, Assistant Keeper of the Queen's Archives, Windsor; Mr D.J.H. Smith of Gloucester Public Record Office; John Munday of the National Maritime Museum; Mr C.R. Hiatt BA, ALA, Gloucester Library; Mr J.R. Wood FLA, AMBIM,

Acknowledgements

Cheltenham Library; Dr Steven Blake, Cheltenham Museum; Stephen Green, the curator at Lords; the historian the Hon. Mrs S. Cubitt OBE; the curators Mr Winder, Mr Lloyd, Mrs V. Moger and Mrs A. Stuart-Smith, all of Hoare's Bank; Sue Heaster, Nottingham University Library; Mrs H.A. Scammell of the Isle of Wight Library; Dudley Jackson; Father Hockey, the writer and historian of Quarr Abbey; Mr D.M. Laverick FLA, Bromley Library; Mr G. Langley BA, FLA, Bristol Central Library; Mr F.I. Whyler, Bromley Historical Society; John Duthie of Aberdeen Art Gallery and Museum; Miss G. Beck, Mrs A. Doughty and Mr B.G. Thomas, all of the County Archives, Guildford; Dr T.R. Thompson FSA, FRHist. Soc., Cricklade Historical Society; Major R.P. Rising RM, Royal Yacht Squadron; Dr Oswald Georg Bauer of the Bayreuthe Festspiele; and Sue Gregory of Trent Polytechnic Library, now Nottingham Trent University.

Specialists in their respective fields who guided me are: the Earl Bathurst; Major-General D.H.G. Rise CBE of the Central Chancery of the Orders of Knighthood; Brigadier P.D. Fabin, Joint Honorary Secretary of the VWH; Mr J. Allen-Stevens MA; Mr K. Dyson, Manager of Nottingham Co-operative Bank; Mr J.C. Daukes, Clerk to the Governing Body, Charterhouse School; Mr J. Moore and Mr S. Cox who advised on points of law; K.R. Arkell and J. Moore, the naval historians; the Revd Ben Hopkinson; Margaret Mann; Mr R. Lindley-Jones; Geoffrey Bond of the Byron Society; Michael Ware, curator of the National Motor Museum, Beaulieu; David Viner, former curator, Cirencester Museum; the researchers Jennie Smith and Valerie Patten; and Dr J. Yorke, FSA, a curator at the V&A and author of *Lancaster House: London's Greatest Town House*, as Stafford House the former home of the Dukes of Sutherland.

I exchanged letters with people on small but important points concerning the history of the *Mercury*. I treasure particularly a brief letter from the late Admiral of the Fleet the Earl Mountbatten of Burma. Similar aid came from Sir George Schuster, Mr C.S.L. Davis of Wadham College, Oxford, Mr A.E.L. Hill, the Rt Revd A.L.E.

Hoskyns-Abrahall and Mr F.W. Penny, formerly an instructor on the ship. I interviewed Mr Mills, also an instructor, just before his death in 1976. Others with whom I exchanged letters are: Mr B.W. Ames, Madeline Attwood, Mrs M. Briggs, Mr A.W. Chaplin, David Cook, Captain A.H. Cooke, Mr H.W. Cookson, Mr P. Dimmick, who taught at the *Mercury* in its closing years, Mr I. Dodd, Mr W. Downing, Cecil Fawcett, Mr J.R. Goudge, George Hoare, Vera Fisher, Josephine Gibbs, the Revd R.L. Hendry, Brenda Hoare, Mrs Hooker, Mr A.F. Jacques, Phyllis Keyte, Mr A.L. Morris, Mr R.C. Payne, Mr and Mrs N. Robinson, Mr B. Stocken, Captain G. Sutton, Zena Thomas, Mabel Whitcombe, Lieutenant-Commander P. Whitlock MBE, a *Mercury* alumnus and a world authority on warships in the days of sail, Mr R.J. Williams, Mr R.S. Wilson, Canon Woodhall, Mr R.S. Wren. The late Sir Frederick Hoare, senior partner in Hoare's Bank, was the first to give me access to the bank's archives and to pass on some of the myths surrounding his remarkable antecedent.

I must make particular mention of the men whose letters covered events at the *Mercury* before, during and after the First World War. They are Mr L.G. Charles, Mr L.A. West, Commander A.H. Horrell RN, Mr R. Sinfield, Captain R.E. Hutchins CBE, DSC, RN, Lieutenant W. Mobsby RN, Mr E.R. Hunter, Mr G.H.F. Prince and Mr E. Walker.

To all the above I express my heartfelt thanks. In several instances the above duplicated material that had already been brought to my attention, but their value was nonetheless welcome as confirmation of that to hand.

I am grateful to the following agencies for permission to quote from works of the authors listed:

Constable & Robinson: the 7th Earl of Bathurst, *A History of the VWH Country*.
Curtis Brown Group Ltd on behalf of the estate of E.W. Swanton, 1972.
HarperCollins: Sir Neville Cardus, *Autobiography*.

Acknowledgements

Michael Hoare: *Margaret Hoare Newspaper Collection (MHNC)*.

Mercury Old Boys' Association, Chairman Captain David Parsons, archive of documents and illustrations.

National Maritime Museum, Greenwich, Manuscripts Manager Daphne Knott, Commander Henry Gardner, *Autobiography*, unpublished.

Orion Publishing Group: Sir Maurice Bowra, *Memories*.

Peter Fraser Dunlop (PFD). J.B. Priestley, *The English* (Copyright © J.B. Priestley, 1973) by permission of PFD on behalf of the estate of J.B. Priestley.

J. Tremlett: family portraits, interview material.

In addition to the above must be listed *C.B. Fry* by Denzil Bachelor, Phoenix House, 1951. All attempts at tracing the copyright holder were unsuccessful.

My final acknowledgement must record the special support given to me by Colin Ridge, Dr Val Benton and especially my brother Norman, who traced and copied many documents and photographs of incalculable value.

The Summer of 1946

The summer of 1946 was magical, with all the variations of weather – sun, wind and rain – following each other in pleasant order, none dominant. On the *Mercury* the fear that was the condition of daily life while Mrs Fry was alive had eased, and when I was told that Captain Fry wanted to see me in his office I had no misgivings. It was my third term on board and I had learned that the one person who would do no harm to a boy was the captain superintendent.

I had been inside The House on several occasions. Mrs Fry had sent for me in the last days of her active rule. I went up to the first-floor room which was the eyrie from which she could see much of what was going on in her domain, and the place where she met the stream of accomplished people, some of whom came at her bidding, writers, adventurers, national leaders, outstanding men who had a story to tell – and who would add to their store once they had met this remarkable – and ultimately tragic – woman.

I have no memory, however, of what she said, for I was afraid, truly afraid, at finding myself in her presence. I have a memory, however, of a large space that had become a picture gallery, its walls crowded with photographs, almost entirely of men, many in uniform, most of them high-ranking officers in the Royal Navy. There was even an overflow of pictures, with screens of the kind used to partition a large space, all of them heavy with the portraits for which there was no room on the walls, more men, the movers and shakers, accustomed to giving orders without qualm that sent the rank and file to their deaths as part of their awesome duties, and of dealing death to the enemies of the nation.

The result of my visit was a spell as pantry boy, who would bring food from the galley that served the whole community and put hot dishes, suitably covered, on a hot plate. There was a hatch in the wall between dining room and pantry. With another boy, who had been in this role for as long as I could remember, I would collect the dirty dishes as they were passed through the hatch to make way for the next course. The pantry was really a long passage, with sinks and draining boards at the end furthest from the hatch. I stationed myself there and would start washing up, but my companion, silent on bare feet, would move back and put his ear to the closed hatch. What I was watching, of course, was the curse of the great house – of any house with servants – the eavesdropper.

Meeting C.B. Fry on his own ground was something else. It was a still day, warm and bright. His door was open and he invited me in at once. The contrast between the two rooms – his wife's and his own – was a contrast of personalities. The one upstairs glorified men of power. The one I had just entered was that of a man who gloried in knowledge. The walls – floor to ceiling – were obscured by books, their titles in gold leaf, and the leather binding having the worn, rather than the frayed, look of years of constant use. The few pictures were of sportsmen, cricketers mostly. His desk was large and covered with books and papers without being untidy. It had a kneehole spacious enough for both of us and he did indeed offer me a chair so that we could sit side by side. There was no typewriter, but there were pens, bottles of ink in different colours, blotting paper and the simple needs of a writer.

I stayed silent and waited for him to speak, just a little nervous at being next to the man in charge, even though he was not giving the orders. Sybil Hoare and Mr Fraser were running the place as if Mrs Fry was still around, waiting for reports. When at last he spoke it was to tell me that my handwriting needed improving. He was quite right, but I was bound to wonder how he knew. I like to think that he did not share in Sybil's habit, still ongoing, of reading our letters, in and out. And since all instruction and teaching was left to those employed for the purpose he could hardly have read the few exercises we did in class. Anyway, he wrote a sentence on a blank sheet of paper, leaving spaces between the lines as you would with a child in the early stages of learning to write. I filled the spaces and he would stop me, take the pen and write over my efforts where I had not been sufficiently precise.

He turned to an entirely different subject when we had filled a page. There were letters on the desk, stamped, addressed and ready to post. He picked one addressed to a national paper, slit it open and pulled out the contents, an article on an aspect of sport. He read it to me, and if I was meant to be impressed, then in truth I was. I had never met a writer before.

After he had read the article he picked up a book. A hardback, it had the title and author in red lettering: *Life Worth Living* by C.B. Fry. 'I want you to read this,' he said. He turned to the window, which was slightly open. 'I'll leave it here, and when you get a spare moment you can pick it up and return it afterwards. If the window is shut, you can easily open it from the outside and help yourself.'

There were few spare moments in a *Mercury* day, the only time in which I could get to read a few pages being in the morning and afternoon breaks when we went to the sports field and lined up to use the heads. There was a shelter and a few seats where we could sit on rainy days while we waited our turn, and I would take the book with me at such times. I didn't enjoy it. There was no story I had spent eight years in boarding schools before I got to the *Mercury* and in the later years I had caught the reading bug and ploughed my way through Dickens, Walter Scott, George Eliot and whatever books I could get my hands on. So I was not without the ability, but I had never read an autobiography before and even the fact of it being recommended by the author was no help.

I never finished it, but it was there at the window for the rest of the term for me to borrow.

For years I wondered why I came to be picked from the row to be given the privilege of a relaxed hour sitting next to one of the most remarkable men of his generation, to be encouraged to read. I believe now that it was a statement, that with his fearsome wife gone he could contemplate the possibility of another kind of school, one where scholarship and intellect would be valued and discipline might take second place to disciplines, where the sneaky devil I met in the pantry would be given short shrift.

ONE

The Mercury

In September 1945 the Training Ship *Mercury* braced itself for a new intake of boys, twenty-five or so, which would be processed into the ranks by those already there. There would be similar intakes after the Christmas and Easter holidays. All would have received a prospectus[1] in which C.B. Fry, the captain superintendent, was listed as joint director with his wife. There were small boarding schools all over the country owned and run by married couples and in most cases the wife would be in charge of the domestic arrangements, a matronly figure who would ensure that pupils were properly fed, accommodated, nursed if need be and made to wash behind their ears. The character and role of the 'matron' in this case was such that some would regret having signed on. The character of the times was such that most would tough it out.

C.B. Fry – such was his fame that the initials were known to everybody, and everybody knew there was only one C.B. – had been at the *Mercury* for thirty-seven years, his varied talents dissipated in an enterprise that might have provided agreeable work for a retired sea captain and half-a-dozen ex-Royal Navy petty officers. What was worse, in the eyes of the limited circle that knew of his situation, was that his captaincy was only nominal. Mrs Fry – one of the most dynamic women of her generation – was in absolute command.

The prospectus that drew a steady stream of boys to the *Mercury* seemed to offer an exciting life in novel surroundings. In a picture of the grounds there was a signal mast of terrifying height, with smiling boys in smart uniform posed on the rigging that held it in place. On the river there was a ship of sorts. She was a 310-foot sloop built for

1

the Royal Navy in 1878 and launched as Her Majesty's Ship (HMS) *Gannet*. Stripped of her masts, rigging and funnel, she had been given an additional deck, and the whole had been roofed over with corrugated iron. To some it looked like a Noah's Ark or a giant houseboat anchored in the middle of the river. To those familiar with life on board she was a descendant of the prison hulks of the time of Dickens. With her gun ports open wide the main deck was massively exposed to the weather, and in winter the upper deck was as cold inside as it was out. Only those who have experienced the British climate with the minimum of protection can appreciate how brutally inhospitable it is for at least six months of the year, and on the ship the *Mercury* boys experienced it at first hand, being spared only the fall of rain and snow directly onto their canvas hammocks.

If there was a warning of hardships to come it was not to be found in the prospectus, but in a strange unsigned letter to the parents of boys headed for the *Mercury*. It began 'Life is a fight from birth to Home'. It was an arresting thought that its author appeared to regard death as Home – adding extra emphasis with a capital letter which mere birth did not warrant. The document went on:

Periods come in everyone's life when it is struggle or slip back, fight or go under; these periods are not incessant in a landsman's life; there is an easing up, a breathing space afforded them when they can survey their position with a certain amount of complacency and safety. Those who take the sea for a career know little of this lull; they admire the sea, they respect the sea, they like the sea, they love the sea, but they have to fight her twenty-four hours of the day. This lifelong fight needs sturdy frames and valiant hearts.

Bodies fit enough to bear extremes of heat and cold; hearts brave enough to take hard knocks and yet stand up again to fight and win.

The TS *Mercury* is not a school; it is not a training school – The *Mercury* is a ship. As a ship she has an atmosphere, a life and a body with a just and kindly heart. The routine is hard; tasks are arduous and discipline strict. Only boys with the sea in their blood can take the life and flourish. The *Mercury* tradition is high. Each boy has it in his own care.

Should your boy be strong enough in body and staunch enough in heart, TS *Mercury* can send him forth to the Seven Seas – very sure of his ability to fight and win.

> . . . and by the vision splendid
> Is on his way attended.

Students of literary style could tell at once that it was not written by C.B., while the content could hardly be the work of a man who, apart from the common enough discomforts of the traditional boarding school, had probably not known a day's real hardship in his life, and whose experience of ships and the sea was nil – if one left aside the occasional trip abroad travelling first-class on an ocean liner. An old sailor might have said that it had been written by someone whose last voyage was on a square-rigged sailing ship – and that so long ago that time had dulled the memory and erased the record of months of boredom that could occur even under sail. Nor did the author realise that boredom was an even greater problem on power-driven ships. Possibly it might have been written by a romantic soul, one who had never had to make a career at sea, but who had been enchanted by the works of Conrad, Melville and Marryat. If it was dishonest or naive about life at sea, it was at least direct in telling parents that life for their sons on the *Mercury* was going to be hell; any lingering doubts in the mind of the new boy about who was in charge were dispelled on his first weekend, for on Saturday Mrs Fry inspected the ship's company, an experience that would leave its members marked for life.

By comparison the appearance of C.B. on Sunday morning for the same purpose was a tame affair. The boys, about 150 of them aged between twelve and sixteen, assembled in two long lines facing each other across a strip of tarmac that ran down one side of the twenty-five room mansion in which C.B. and his wife lived. Mercury House was always referred to as The House. C.B. appeared before them at about ten o'clock in his uniform of Honorary Captain in the Royal Naval Reserve. Occasionally he would wear his greatcoat with the collar turned up, arousing the suspicion that it hid the informal garb of somebody taken against his will from a quiet Sunday morning with the papers.

At seventy-three C.B. Fry was the epitome of dignified old age – erect, clear-eyed and relaxed. Those who tried to describe a man who had spent half a century in the public eye often employed the word 'patrician'. If hackneyed, it was appropriate. There was in the aristocratic profile the restrained hauteur of one who wanted to appear confident in noble lineage, with every assurance that his account of himself, could modesty be waived, would reveal one who was a gentleman with the best credentials, an expensive education at an ancient school, years at university, and a distinguished career. His air was essentially that of the amateur whose skills were concealed and who would only exercise them publicly with reluctance, but then with an *élan* that would dismay the professional. Such a figure should have excited awe, perhaps even fear and blind devotion. He was accorded instead the benign admiration given to a retired sportsman.

C.B. would screw his monocle into his right eye and allow himself to be steered along the lines by one of his staff as if he were a distinguished visitor arriving at an airport and obliged to inspect a Guard of Honour before leaving for lunch at Buckingham Palace. It was brief, but it was harmless when contrasted with what had taken place the previous day.

On Saturday the boys would assemble in the same place to be inspected by Mrs Fry. They brought with them their entire meagre kit, each one making a neat pile on the ground of spare uniform, marching and football boots, wet-weather oilskins, overalls and toothbrush. Incongruously, there rested on top of the piles a handkerchief that each boy had had for a week and was damp as a result of his having scrubbed it on the floor of the showers earlier that morning. There had been three hours of frantic preparation to get all this ready, with brief interruptions to go to the showers, breakfast and chapel. Fear, hunger, cold and fatigue were the prime elements in the lives of these boys, but never was fear more apparent than on this morning when they would come face-to-face with Mrs Fry.

Less frightened, perhaps, but suitably respectful of the lady, was the staff of instructors. They too would be on parade at the moment she appeared, some of them grouped in front of a small clock tower at one end of the tarmac, the others between the lines of boys. Those between the lines were called watch officers, the equivalent of housemasters in other schools.

The staff consisted of seven or eight men who were referred to as officers, though none of them had held officer status in either the armed forces or the Merchant Navy. For the most part they were ex-petty officers of the Royal Navy, the hard men of the lower deck who looked ill-at-ease in uniforms with one or two gold rings on their sleeves in near-imitation of those worn by officers of the Royal Navy. More at ease in their uniforms, and infinitely more skilled in their subject, were the bandmasters, a trio of men whose professionalism and numbers – three to teach music where only one taught seamanship – showed the weight attached to music in the curriculum. The senior man wore three rings. He was a short, broad-shouldered man of craggy good looks with a pleasant husky voice and an unmistakable air of command, though he too had never been an officer. Harold Fraser was styled the Chief Officer, and had been on the staff for over twenty years.

At ten o'clock Fraser looked about him for the last time before going into The House to fetch Mrs Fry, leaving the company standing at ease, waiting. When he returned he was still alone. He came out of the door, went to a point in the middle of the narrow parade ground and turned around. A minute or so later, slowly but steadily, walking stick in hand, the ruler of this gathering emerged. Fraser called everybody to attention and raised his right hand to his cap in salute. His colleagues did the same. The look on his face never varied. It was that mixture of awe, fear and blind devotion that her husband so signally failed to inspire.

Mrs Fry's first act was to nod to the men near the clock tower and wish them 'Good morning' in a deep gruff voice. The men saluted again and departed, leaving behind the watch officers and Mr Fraser.

Mrs Fry wore a uniform of sorts. Her navy-blue double-breasted jacket was modelled on those of her staff, with eight buttons. It had the two larger pockets of the male jacket but no breast pocket. Above where the pocket should have been she wore the ribbon of the OBE. Just visible below an ankle-length skirt were thick woollen stockings and brightly polished black shoes, each topped with a silver buckle. There were superstitions attached to the colour of the stockings: red if she was in a bad mood, yellow if her mood was good. More often than not she wore red. Her hat was round with a high crown and a wide brim, and the thick band of material round the crown carried a brass badge. Under her jacket she wore a man's white shirt and a black tie. Thick leather gloves completed the costume. Judging by the antiquated style and faded material, it was the very same uniform that she had worn in 1927 when the then Prince of Wales had visited the ship, and again in 1929 when his brother, the Duke of York, later King George VI, had spent the day there.

She was now eighty-three. Her ancient face was deeply lined and she had a thin bloodless mouth of jolting severity. Pale little moles on her cheeks sprouted grey hairs. She was of average height, but men who remembered her in younger days described her as a big woman whose progress through the day was that of a great ship under full sail, so formidable was her presence. In spite of her years she squared her shoulders like the boys she was about to inspect and held her head in a faintly arrogant tilt.

'Where shall we begin, Mr Fraser?'

This was said in a measured way, the words spaced out as if they were some sort of currency, and hard currency at that, to be dispensed grudgingly and to the maximum possible effect. She could produce fear in a boy, and probably in a man too, with a long steady look, followed by two words of censure that left him quaking.

Fraser took her to the first boy in one of the long rows and began the business of picking over the piles of kit set neatly on the ground. For up to two hours she moved steadily up and down the lines looking intently at hundreds of garments. The Chief Officer hovered at her shoulder, notebook in hand, deeply anxious that everything should be to her satisfaction. If things were not so, he scribbled the details on a page and looked at the offender in a meaningful way. A resistant stain, a button loose, a boot inadequately laced counted as capital crimes. With naval precision, each item was picked up to an exact rhythm and similarly replaced. There were curious rituals that were unknown outside the *Mercury* – certainly not in Divisions, the inspection carried out in naval establishments of which this exercise was supposed to be an equivalent. The boys had, for example, to bend down in unison and pull up their trouser legs for Mrs Fry to inspect their bootlaces. Then another order was shouted in the strangled voice peculiar to parade grounds, the last word exploding into the air like a hand grenade going off: 'Pick up toothbrushes and *handkerchiefs*!' They went down again and came upright holding the named items, damp hankie in the left hand, toothbrush in the right. On the order 'Show teeth!' they held out the left hand in a mad parody of a Nazi salute and brought up the right so that the toothbrush reposed, bristles outwards, against the bottom lip. At the same time they bared their front teeth, and once again the slow progress took place and each boy was minutely examined.

Never in her progress did she speak directly to a boy, and to be the object of her attention was deeply frightening. When she stopped in front of one her face was a mask. If it showed any feeling at all it was of quiet disdain. She would look him in the face, a look it was dangerous to return, and address herself to Mr Fraser. She spoke with the languid drawl of the very rich and very confident upper class.

7

'Who is this boy?'

'Three – five – seven – eight.' He spoke each digit carefully as they were known only by their numbers, even among themselves.

'Tell him to take his hat off.'

'Three – five – seven – eight, off hat.'

'Turn him round.'

'About turn.'

'I don't like the look of that boy at all, Mr Fraser.'

It was a pronouncement that could make a boy sick with apprehension, for in addition to the punishments she could ordain, sometimes for no better reason than her dislike of a boy, there was the wrath of his companions who could be expected to suffer since she might condemn not just the one bad apple but the whole barrel.

Mrs Fry had strong views about hair. Style did not matter since nobody had any. It was clipped to the skin on her orders. Approaching holiday time a boy's hair might have grown a luxuriant inch that he hoped he could keep. He did not want to appear in his own streets with a stubbled pate, the hallmark in those days of men and boys who had been in trouble with the law. Some believed she ordered it to be cut so as to send one home bearing the stamp of her control.

It is a characteristic of the young that they cannot envisage the elderly, with their grey hair, lined faces and bodies wilting with age, as having been young, bold and passionate beings like themselves. For *Mercury* boys in particular it was unimaginable that the woman who treated them so coldly, whose eagle-eyed inspections they dreaded, had been brought before them by a chain of events set in motion by an explosion of passion, of blind indiscipline, when she was much their age. It was an explosion that devastated the lives and fortunes of all around her.

When it was all over, and the grim, mirthless, ancient lady had returned to The House, there was a universal feeling of relief, almost of euphoria. The boys cleared everything away and went light-heartedly on to the next piece of routine, a gruelling hour of drill on the playing field with old Lee Enfield rifles and bayonets.

There were other aspects of life on the ship, if such were needed, that stamped indelibly on the minds of all present the power over their lives of the woman in command. No one owned a hairbrush for the obvious reason that no one had hair to brush. No one needed nail clippers or scissors. Finger- and toenails were ground down by the constant scrubbing and cleaning which were features of daily life. The boys went barefoot winter and summer, wearing boots only for parades and inspections and on dry evenings when they marched to the pier on their way to the dormitory ship; on wet evenings they tied their boots together by the laces and hung them round their necks. Gloves and scarves were not part of the uniform, and hats were seldom worn. Most buildings were either unheated or poorly heated. The only warmth to be had came from vigorous activity, and a dreaded punishment was to be made to stand motionless on a cold day next to a flagstaff near The House. No one told them that these hardships had been instituted by Mrs Fry sixty years earlier when she was a vigorous young woman in her early twenties, most of which she had endured herself along with those on whom she had inflicted them.

To the discomforts of bare feet and the general hardships of everyday life at the *Mercury* were added restrictions that made it seem like a prison for those inside, one with an open gate, but almost impossible to escape. Repeatedly during the day the order was given to 'Muster All Hands', to count heads and account for everybody not present. If a boy decided to run away he would have little more than half-an-hour's start before he was missed, an hour at the most.

At nine o'clock every evening the boys prepared to go to the dormitory ship. A group went ahead of the main body, going out by dinghy to fetch two cutters from their moorings on the river and bring them to the pier for the rest to get into. Life-jackets were never worn; there wasn't one in the place, and if a boat had gone down the loss of life would have been appalling. Booted and wearing heavy oilskins over the denim overalls they were going to need at 'Clean Ship' the following morning, they would never have stood a chance if a grossly overladen cutter had succumbed to the ferocity of a winter's gale bellowing up the Hamble. Yet they took the risk without a thought, made nonchalant by repetition and the simple necessity of having to get to where they could sleep. Life had indeed been lost over the years. Tied up to the ship was a seldom-used cutter called the *Maurice Driver* after a boy who had gallantly, but fruitlessly, dived into the river one black night to bring back a shipmate who had fallen overboard.

They piled into the boats, so many of them packed so tightly in the stern-sheets, under the rowing benches and in the bows, that the gunwales – the upper sides of the boats – were barely clear of the water. Only in the most violent storms was thought given to the possibility that this might be dangerous, and more journeys made by a cutter with fewer people on board and a specially picked rough-weather crew on the oars.

The shipboard routine could be simple and quick. On the main deck, in spaces between the guns, the boys assembled in four groups, thirty-seven to a group, two to starboard and two to port, facing inboard. Within each group were three sections of twelve, with their section leaders at their head. The whole was called a watch, and had a leading hand in charge.

The first job was to get the hammocks slung. Half of the company, consisting mainly of the older boys, went to the upper deck and the rest to the orlop deck, much of which was below the waterline and thus marginally the warmer of the two in winter.

The hammocks slung, the boys returned to the main deck, undressed and got into pyjamas. At this moment they could never be sure that the logical next step would take place whereby the roll would be called and, after some unusual bits of ritual, they would all be dismissed to their hammocks. Once in a while, the duty officer was moved to assert himself in a way that reminded everybody that he was very much in charge; and since on still nights the sounds of activity on the ship, including much shouting of orders and loud bugle calls, carried to The House, the people there would get the message too. As long as he did not hit anyone he could be as severe as he liked.

On this particular night Mr Stark is on duty. The boys are assembled on the main deck, shivering in the cold air blasting through the open gun ports. Mr Stark stands amidships, the bugler close at hand, and looks about for an excuse to administer a 'shake-up', the term used to describe the flurry of excessive discipline demanded by Mrs Fry when she imagines the boys are getting slack. He announces that the exercise of slinging hammocks was too noisy and took too long.

In the apprehensive silence that follows he walks to the ship's bell at the fore end of the main deck and rings it briskly – the signal for 'Fire Stations'. The boys explode into action. In seconds they have closed the gun ports, covered various hatches and done a score of jobs connected with the exercise. Mr Stark shouts,

'Bugler! Sound the "Still".' The four ascending notes have an electric effect. There is instant silence. Everybody freezes.

'Fire starboard side for'ard!' he shouts.

'Carry on!'

Two more notes on the bugle and pandemonium is resumed.

A hose is run out, one end is clamped to a rotary pump on the after deck and the other fitted with a nozzle and pointed through an opening in the ship's side near the mythical fire. More orders follow, each emphasised by a bugle call.

'Heave round!'

Four boys seize the pump handle and swing it round with gusto. The hose fills and little drops of water appear on its surface that hang momentarily and then slide off to form pools on the deck. The jet of water shoots from the nozzle and soon a sound as of heavy rain drifts back to the ship as it falls on the surface of the darkened river.

'Vast heaving!'

The pump stops and the tired, angry, helpless company waits in suspense for the next order. At this late hour, when 'Last Post' should long since have sounded and the rows of stretched hammocks received their exhausted burdens, will he go the whole way? He does.

'Abandon ship!'

11

There is a rush to the boats, and in seconds the ship's company, clad only in pyjamas, is afloat. Only the bugler and Mr Stark remain on board.

'Take your boats round the ship and return on board,' he shouts into the darkness.

Back on board it takes ten minutes to mop up the mess of the fire drill, hang up wet lengths of hose, reopen the gun ports and get the routine back to the point at which it had been interrupted when Mr Stark rang the bell. Now follows a moment of ritual that must make him wince every time he comes to it. He is a middle-aged ex-petty officer, demobilised in the closing weeks of the Second World War, who has spent most of his working life in the Royal Navy. He has survived the boring years of peace and the years on foreign stations. He has survived the hell of the North Atlantic and the double hell of the Russian convoys, when German ships and aircraft had battered his ship, and when – according to legend – he had often picked up the bloody remains of a casualty, put them in a bucket and unceremoniously dumped them into the sea so that the living could get on with the business of survival. Coarsened by his experiences, he must nevertheless set in train a quasi-religious ritual which is part of his job at the *Mercury*, the best job he has ever had for the excellent reason that it is on a ship that is going nowhere. If he appears to be losing his touch, it's the sack and back to real ships again and all the hardships he has escaped. Mrs Fry knows that for every man she employs there are thousands queuing behind him for similar work where they can use their nautical skills without having to go to sea. For this reason her staff live in fear of her and do exactly as she says.

'Port Watches, about turn!'

With this order Mr Stark brings the boys who had their backs to the pier facing in that direction along with those on the starboard side of the ship.

'Kneel.'

All go down on their knees. There is a flutter of hands as the few Roman Catholics in the ranks cross themselves. For two minutes they stay there in utter silence, perhaps the first real silence there has been that day. Some kneel uncomplainingly on the damp patches made by the fire hose. By now all are past caring about the bone-chilling cold.

Mr Stark can be forgiven for pondering the meaning of this part of the evening ritual, wondering to what extent they are being asked to kneel and address themselves to their Maker, and how much of it is an obeisance to the people in The House (which everybody is obliged to face). Perhaps it crosses his mind that they are like adherents of a religious sect whose prayers will have no weight unless they are made in a prescribed direction.

'Stand. Bugler, sound the note.'

A solitary, note is given, and they sing:

> So be our rest Thy palaces most fair,
> Not built with hands, whose stones Thy praise declare,
> Where war is not, and all Thy sons are free,
> Where Thou art known, and all is known in Thee.

Presumably Mr Stark is aware of the irony. They sing of celestial palaces, freedom and a knowingness beyond all human understanding when he has subjected them in this austere barrack of a ship to an attack on even that little freedom left to them, the freedom to escape in sleep from the hardships of the day, and all for reasons beyond their comprehension.

The singing carries across the water, across the reeds by the riverbank and up to an open window on the first floor of The House. In deep chairs by the window two women sit listening – Mrs Fry and a Miss Hoare who is in her early sixties, about whom the boys know nothing except that she bears the surname of the man who founded the *Mercury* in 1885.

They heard the commands, the bugle calls, and now they hear the singing. They heard, no doubt with satisfaction, the change in the routine that they had established. They hear the final bugle call of the day, 'Last Post', and then watch as the lights on the ship go out, one by one. At last they too prepare for sleep, satisfied that they are still in absolute command of the most remarkable school in England.

In another part of The House C.B. lies in bed, not asleep, but staring at the ceiling as he recites aloud a ball-by-ball account of a cricket match that took place half a century earlier.

TWO

The Young Adventurers

The year 1885 was not only that in which Charles Hoare founded the *Mercury*. It was also the year in which he appeared in a London court with a young woman to answer charges arising out of his long affair with her, beginning when she was barely into her teens, when Charles was twice her age, married, and the father of five children. The young woman was Beatrice Holme Sumner – Beatie to her family – and later Mrs Fry. Their origins and his means were such that their presence in the Court of Chancery and the likelihood of a prison sentence were almost unbelievable. At risk with them were several of Beatie's relatives, most notably her cousin, Winifred Ida, Lady Cholmondeley, wife of the Marquess of Cholmondeley, Joint Hereditary Great Chamberlain of England and thus one of the figures closest to the monarch. It was an event that ravaged the lives of people close to them, and left many others socially embarrassed.

Beatie was born on 12 July 1862 at Hatchlands, a well-appointed mansion in Surrey not many miles south of London. An ancestor, William Brightwell Sumner, had purchased the house from the widow of Admiral Boscawen in the previous century, and her father, Arthur Sumner, had inherited it. The Sumners had been rich merchants, landowners, academics and churchmen. One had been Provost of King's College, Cambridge, another Archbishop of Canterbury. Beatie's Aunt Georgiana, her father's sister, was married to Lord Fitzhardinge of Berkeley Castle, and her mother's sister was a Kingscote from the village of the same name in Gloucestershire. When *Mercury* boys lined up outside The House on Saturday mornings it was to be inspected by a woman who was descended

15

through the Kingscotes from the Kings of England and of Denmark. Lady Godiva, she who rode naked though the streets of Coventry in protest at the heavy taxes imposed by her husband, was in her family tree. The relatives in whose houses she and her parents were welcome guests included the Dukes of Beaufort and of Richmond, Lord Bathurst and Lord Curzon, and her cousins could be discovered in many of the great country houses of the British Isles.

Little is known about Beatie's early life, for much of the evidence was destroyed in a bonfire of her papers and pictures immediately after her death. Tales told at second and third hand by descendants of the Kingscote, Sumner and Hoare families suggest that from an early age she was remarkable for her strong will and defiant nature, and almost impossible to control. The conventions of Victorian society dictated that she should be given over to a nanny and a governess, who would combine to teach her manners and the limited range of skills and subjects deemed suitable preparation for a girl whose aim in life was a suitable marriage, the rearing of children and discreet idleness. In an unsettled childhood Beatie escaped these measures, and instead of learning to read she learned to ride, spending as much time as possible with horses. Her command of them mirrored the command she exercised at home, where servants, many of them mature men and women, were subordinate to their employer's children. From an early age Beatie had what might be best described as natural arrogance, a sense of power over others that surpassed mere belief or conviction.

By the time she was twelve she had the reputation of an adventurer, of being a distinctive personality with an insistent nature, vivacious, enthusiastic and impulsive. Poorly educated, she had nevertheless the capacity to apply herself with terrifying single-mindedness to whatever she thought important. Those who have read the biography by Mrs Alexander of Jane Welsh Carlyle, wife of the well-known essayist, historian and philosopher, will be struck by the description of Jane and how close it comes to a description of Beatie at the same age – fiery, strong-willed, aggressive, not above punching someone who got in the way, and utterly fearless.

Documentation of Beatie's life begins in her early teens, by which time she was disturbingly mature. Women were dismayed at the attention she drew from their menfolk. At about this time she achieved what C.B. Fry's biographer, Denzil Batchelor, described as 'an unusual double'.[1] She was made an honorary whip of the Duke of Beaufort's Hounds, and was the model for a painting by G.F. Watts, the distinguished Victorian artist, a tribute to her as a 'celebrated beauty'.[2] She was, however, handsome rather than beautiful, with a high forehead that, in later years, she emphasised by wearing her hair very short. She had calm eyes that looked steadily at people, seeming to see more of their personalities than they would have liked to give away. Her mouth was firm with lips much fuller than one would expect in a woman who, in old age, was noted for her thin, aggressive mouth. Her straight nose and a chin that jutted slightly completed a face that was full of determination and strength of character.

The placid Gloucestershire countryside of the mid-1870s was stirred by her appearance in the hunting field; the great hunt clubs of the area – the Beaufort, the Vale of White Horse (known to everybody as the 'VWH'.) and the Cotswold – had an unusually large turnout of members who wanted to see her in action as she rode with courage and skill far beyond her years. An incident in her final years suggests that she wore jodhpurs and rode astride rather than side saddle, and this alone would have attracted attention. She had, in fact, a penchant for manly garb that lasted for life.

While little is known of Beatie the child, even less is known of her parents. Her mother seemed to have been an inadequate and pathetic woman whose ill judgement in the matter of her daughter's conduct fuelled the disaster that was to envelop the whole family, her father pale, ineffectual and insufficiently forceful to stand up to her. Both parents, it is said, were torn between pride in her riding accomplishments and despair at their inability to control her. Their grip on Beatie's young life was further diminished when Mrs Sumner found that her daughter could be more decisive and shrewder than herself in domestic matters. One cannot discipline a child one moment and then consult her the next without some loss of authority.

Beatie was living with her parents in Cheltenham when her appearance and her extraordinary character began to draw attention. The family had arrived in the town in 1874 after spending the previous five years on the move. A downturn in their fortunes had left them unable to maintain their home and the standard of living they preferred and they were obliged to live on the income from renting Hatchlands to other people, notably Count Haryett de Bechevet and his Hungarian wife Marianne.

The five years of wandering may well have proved traumatic to a girl reared in a stately home. From 1869, when Beatie was only seven, the lofty rooms and corridors of her birthplace, the lush gardens, the broad parkland beyond – all were exchanged for a series of rented houses in the towns and cities of Gloucestershire. Where there had been stability of place, with a predictable calendar of events, familiar social exchanges and loyal servants constantly on hand, there were now uncertainties, the repeated need to reassert themselves at each new address. In the highly stratified society of late nineteenth-century England they must have been all too aware of the gulf between their way of life and that of noble relatives still secure in their country houses and castles. If nobility has its obligations, it also has its disadvantages. Beatie's father could not make money in ways unbecoming to a gentleman. Although he was an authority on farm animals, in demand as a judge at the county agricultural shows of the day where he shared the duties with men like the Duke of Beaufort and Charles Hoare, it would have been considered beneath him to trade in the cattle market, turning his expertise to good account by buying and selling animals in competition with auctioneers, dealers and butchers. Yet he desperately needed the money. In Cheltenham he became Master of the Cotswold Hunt, a post that required a large private income if he was to satisfy the expectations of the club members, and he did so against mounting debts. The uneducated Beatie had been acquiring an education of sorts, of the kind that would never have been granted her had she remained sheltered into her teens in the elegant surroundings of Hatchlands. She had been made tough and decisive, and could handle people in ways that went beyond merely being 'good with servants'.

Beatie Sumner met Charles Hoare – appropriately enough – on the hunting field, though stories that survived for over a century would have had people believe otherwise. Her good looks and precocity drew the attention of men to the extent that they forgot they were meeting someone who was still a child. It was said that Charles was invited to meet her at Berkeley Castle, where his hosts, Lord and Lady Fitzhardinge, would turn a blind eye while he made heavy overtures to Beatie, perhaps to the point of seducing her. This, it was hoped, would frighten her off men – a necessary step, her relatives thought, since she was obviously enjoying the effect she had on the opposite sex. The plot failed, the story goes, when Beatie seduced her would-be seducer. As will be seen, the story of any meeting between Charles and Beatie at Berkeley is so improbable that it is surprising that it survived so long; but there may be a germ of truth in the belief that Beatie was the dominant partner in the relationship. She was still short of her fifteenth birthday when her father was first moved to upbraid Charles for his ardent pursuit of the girl. Beatie, significantly, did nothing to discourage her admirer.

Charles was born on 18 May 1847, at a house in Birdcage Walk, London, the son of Peter Richard Hoare, a partner in Hoare's Bank, Fleet Street. His mother was Lady Sophia, daughter of Lord Romney, the 2nd Earl. Their home was Kelsey Manor, Beckenham, on the outskirts of London, described by an estate agent when it came on the market at the end of the century as 'suitable for a nobleman or gentleman of fortune'.[3] Charles was to inherit this and a great deal more besides. His childhood, however, was spent not at Kelsey but at Luscombe Castle in Devon, another of his father's properties and equally grand.

Luscombe Castle was Charles's home and the school in which he was to be groomed for high office in the family business. But he was no scholar. An account of his boyhood says that he had little taste for the classics, literature and the gentler arts, 'the constraints of ordered boyhood being abhorrent to him. His school was the Devonshire fields, his university the world.'⁴ Others describe his childhood in less charitable terms, with touches that suggest a startling resemblance to Beatie's early life. He was an impossible child – self-willed, riding roughshod over all attempts to have him conform. He may have been spared the routine of his class, of being sent to an exclusive school such as Eton or Harrow, because he was slightly lame or, as Beatie later described it, 'he walked a little late'.

His lameness may have been at the root of his brilliance as a sportsman. He drove himself to excel in sport in defiance of his handicap, especially in cricket, playing on equal terms with professionals. Cricket was a lifelong passion, one that was to bring him into contact with C.B. Fry. The young C.B., playing near his Chislehurst home in Kent in the 1890s, inevitably met the aging Charles who freely spent his money to entertain the stars of the sport he loved. Charles also excelled at tennis, but above all at horsemanship. Mounted, his disability vanished; he looked and felt supremely confident, and in time came to be acknowledged as one of the finest riders in the country. He grew into a big bear of a man, over six feet tall, with no taste for banking, but with a vast appetite for the good things in life – by which he meant property, horses and yachts – which his stake in the bank and his subsequent inheritance could pay for. The yachts were largely for show, the trappings of wealth, though there is a report of his wife spending a holiday on one in the Mediterranean and having to be towed into Marseilles when it was becalmed. One was moored at Exmouth and was used to train local boys who then found jobs on other private yachts. A few went into the Royal Navy.

When Charles and Beatie met they must have felt the rapport of people whose experiences, personalities, drives and skills were in many respects identical. Like was attracted to like, it appeared, with irresistible urgency. There were, however, certain obstacles. In 1867 Charles had married Margaret Baring Short, of Bickham House in

Devon. Curiously, though Luscombe Castle and Bickham were not many miles apart, his letter asking for an interview with Mr Baring Short to discuss marriage with Margaret was addressed from a nearby hotel, and for the rest of his life Luscombe hardly featured in his travels.

On the surface the two young people were well matched. Both had titled relatives and ancestors; both were predictably well off and able to move among their peers with all the self-assurance of the Victorian upper classes.

The differences between them, however, were considerable. Charles was a man for the outdoors, happy to spend every day of the long hunting season in the saddle, and turning to his yachts, to cricket and to tennis in the summer. When he went to London it was to enjoy life at Boodle's, the exclusive club in St James, rather than the theatre and concerts, and there is little to suggest that he read anything other than the popular papers and journals.

Margaret, by contrast, was a petite, pretty woman, more cerebral in her pleasures. A portrait of her as a young woman suggests a shy person, with a wide forehead and gentle eyes. Her boldest features were her dark hair and black arching eyebrows. Her first love was music. She had a rich contralto voice and appeared in concerts that she organised with her friends to raise money for charities. Mozart was her favourite composer, judging from the programmes. If Margaret and Charles had any taste in common it lay in their appreciation of furniture, paintings and antiques, with Charles specialising in nautical artefacts such as ship models of the great men-o'-war of previous centuries.

They had five sons and a daughter, but one son died after an accident in which he broke his neck.

It was soon after their marriage that Charles came into the public eye, as becomes apparent from Margaret's scrapbook of cuttings that spanned thirty years of their lives and ran to over a thousand items. Unfortunately most of the items are undated, nor is it clear what newspapers and journals they are from, but the collection is remarkable for its candour. One of the earliest cuttings tells of the unfortunate experience of a 'notorious speculator' on the stock exchange. Legend has it that the 'speculator' was her husband. It is worth quoting in full:

> One of the current topics of 'Town' gossip is the tremendous failure of the younger member of a well-known banking firm who has 'gone' for the enormous sum of £400,000 on the Stock Exchange. The young man was some little time ago a rather warm patron of the Turf, and showed some disposition to 'plunge' in a mild sort of way. The senior partner feared that if it came to the ears of the public that one of the firm was in any way connected with the Turf it might affect their credit for respectability, so at their request the young man abandoned the Turf and took to gambling on the Stock Exchange, with the happy result I have named.[5]

At the beginning of the twenty-first century the equivalent of £400,000 lost in the 1860s would translate into millions.

Most of the earliest cuttings filed by Margaret deal with the revival of coaching and of her husband's part in it. After the rapid spread of railways there grew up nostalgia for the days of coaches with teams of horses and all the colourful paraphernalia that went with them. The prime mover in this was the Duke of Beaufort, who started a joint stock company in the summer of 1866 with shares of £10 each. Significantly for Charles's fortunes, most of the shareholders came from Gloucestershire. A coach called *Old Times* was put on the old mail road from Brighton to the London terminus in Piccadilly. The twenty-year-old Charles put his own coach, *Exquisite*, on the road in 1867. The coach owners did not merely finance them – they occasionally drove them as well, vying with each other in their skill as coachmen, in smartness of appearance, and in the promptness with which the schedules were maintained.

The start of the coaching season became a social occasion, widely reported in the London papers. On one such occasion the Prince of Wales occupied a box seat of the Duke of Beaufort's family coach.

The passengers included the Countess of Westmoreland and Lady Emily Kingscote. Ironically, it was Lady Emily's husband who was to put Charles into the Court of Chancery where he was threatened with imprisonment for his affair with Beatie Sumner, a niece of the Kingscotes.

As Margaret Hoare's collection of newspaper cuttings grew, it came to include, at first by chance, and then by design, the names of people who had two things in common: they came from the Gloucestershire hunting world, and they would feature in one of the greatest scandals of Victorian times, a scandal that was to break up her marriage. She even filed reports that hinted at her husband's infidelities.

THREE

Huntsman and Huntress

Beatie was fifteen in 1877 when Charles finally abandoned coaching in Kent for the hunting scene in Gloucestershire. He was now very rich indeed, having been made a senior partner of Hoare's Bank. If his attentions to the girl were to give offence to her father, they were to prove almost as unpalatable to Lord Bathurst, the 6th Earl. In the tight, closed world of their class it is not surprising to find that girl and earl were related, Sumners and Bathursts having married into the Hankey family in the previous century.

Lord Bathurst, who lived in Cirencester, had at first welcomed Charles to the county and encouraged him to become Master of the VWH in succession to Lord Shannon.

Hunting in the nineteenth century was a robust and sometimes violent world that functioned not only as a social bond for the landowners across whose country it took place, but also as a training ground for the military and an arena in which deep friendships were formed and private vendettas fought out. It was in some instances a statement of just how few were those who did indeed own the land. It was said that the Berkeley family, more of Beatie's relatives, could hunt all the way from Berkeley Castle to Berkeley Square in London without leaving their property, a distance of nearly one hundred miles.

Bathurst estates were also extensive. More important, however, were the family connections. From far back in their history they had been confidants and secret service agents to monarchs. Their ranks included members of Parliament and holders of high government offices. Henry, the 2nd Earl, was Lord Chancellor and his son Henry was Secretary of State for War and Colonies for fifteen years at the time of Waterloo. In the late eighteenth century Sir Benjamin Bathurst was a governor of the East India Company as well as Treasurer to Queen Anne, who created his son, Allen, 1st Lord Bathurst in 1711. Although they had financial dealings with Hoare's Bank, Charles, by their standards, was not a serious figure.

In the 1920s the 7th Earl of Bathurst wrote a history of the VWH Hunt. Reflecting on the turbulent relationship between his father and Charles Hoare, he said:

It was an unlucky day on which Mr. C.A.R. Hoare was elected Master of the V.W.H., for his mastership led to all sorts of social difficulties as well as extreme friction between land-owners and farmers in the country. Mr. Hoare was a big, stout, rather common-looking man. He was rich, having been a partner in Hoare's Bank. He set himself up as being a great sportsman, and a coaching man, and probably looked his best in a big box-cloth coat, driving either a four-in-hand, or a pair of horses in a mail phaeton.[1]

In a footnote Lord Bathurst added, 'He was nicknamed "The Coachman".'[2]

The Coachman's first home in Gloucestershire was Easton Grey House, five miles from the Duke of Beaufort's home at Badminton and six from that of Colonel Kingscote. The Colonel lived in Kingscote village with an estate large enough to include a private racecourse. Cirencester, the heart of VWH country, was fourteen miles away, an exquisite town with many properties of Cotswold stone that accorded them an instant patina of age and dignity regardless of when they were built. Charles's connections in the country were already strong, dating back to his coaching days in London. Yet they were more than merely sporting connections. When the daughter of Henry Van Notten Pole married Reginald Herbert in 1875 the ceremony took place in a church in Fulham Road, London, and the reception at the Ranelagh Club nearby.

Bride and groom departed for a honeymoon at Kelsey Park, Beckenham, 'the picturesque and charming seat of Mr C.A.R. Hoare'.[3] Many of those they left behind came from Gloucestershire. The Duke and Duchess of Beaufort headed the list of guests.

There is nothing to suggest that Charles's move to Gloucestershire and his wish to take over the VWH from Lord Shannon were in any way connected with his passion for Beatie Sumner, but being the Master of one of the foremost hunt clubs in country bordering on that in which Beatie's father was Master made it easy for the two to meet under the guise of a shared passion for the sport rather than for one another. It may have been chance. Hindsight makes it look like design.

When Charles succeeded Lord Shannon in 1879 he did so on a wave of goodwill from the whole countryside, bringing as he did a reputation for sportsmanship and the kind of wealthy patronage needed to make for successful hunting. Even Arthur Sumner, in spite of Charles's over-attentiveness to Beatie, welcomed the new Master to his table and joined cheerfully in a toast to 'the Neighbouring Hunts' when the Cotswold and the VWH dined together that year. Sumner returned the visit and attended a VWH puppy show. It was a wet day. The puppies had been judged, luncheon served in a marquee next to the Cirencester kennels, and the prizes awarded. In view of the heavy rain, Charles, as Chairman, suggested 'a little harmony to pass away the time till the weather saw fit to mend'.[4] And so the hunt club members sang to each other – hunting songs and old English ballads. In a lull in the music, Sumner made an impromptu speech in which he observed amid cheers that it would be wrong for them to separate without thanking and drinking the health of their generous and popular host.

However, the shadows were lengthening. That same year, it became necessary to move Beatie from Cheltenham, so ardent had Charles become in pursuit of the girl. A Southampton paper described how he was caught in her bedroom 'in circumstances which he could not satisfactorily explain'. Beatie's father and her uncle, Colonel Kingscote, brought her and Charles together and demanded a pledge that they would no longer meet or communicate with each other in any way. So uncertain were they that the lovers would honour this pledge that they persuaded Lord and Lady Fitzhardinge to take Beatie into Berkeley Castle. The castle was then, as it is now, an unusual and splendid house that had developed within the walls of a great fortress. There was no suggestion of Beatie being locked up in a tower like the heroine of a romantic novel. It was hoped, however, that all her activities could be monitored more closely in a place which was remote from town life, where there were no busy streets into which a precocious girl could disappear on her own private errands.

Even today Berkeley Castle is remote: witness the construction of a nuclear power station within sight of the castle, between it and the River Severn. With few outside distractions Beatie would have fallen into the routine of family life, including attendance of the village church that stands close to the fortified entrance to the castle. She would go from the castle proper into the inner courtyard, through massive gates into the outer to follow a low wall on her left over which she could see green fields and dark woods stretching to the horizon with hardly another human habitation in sight, all of it the property of the people with whom she was staying. Inside the church she would be seated near impressive reminders of her ancestry, fifteenth-century tombs of the Berkeleys, the 11th Earl and his son, side-by-side, in armour, their hands pressed piously together, their feet resting on lions – symbols of courage in battle. Close to the altar she would see the grave of Edward Jenner, the discoverer of vaccination. Miles away in Kingscote village church a notice in the porch reads:

> Edward Jenner 1749–1823 was married in this church to Catharine Kingscote 6 March 1788. His marriage brought him much happiness.

Wherever she went in Gloucestershire she would see these reminders of the powerful and influential people with whom she was connected.

If further reminder was needed it came on 16 July, four days after Beatie's seventeenth birthday. Dressed in cream-coloured India muslin trimmed with lace, with a hat to match, she was one of ten bridesmaids at the wedding of her cousin Winifred Ida Kingscote to Lord Rocksavage, soon to become Marquess of Cholmondeley as his father and grandfather died in quick succession. The ceremony took place in St George's, Hanover Square, one of London's 'fashionable' churches. It began promptly at 3 o'clock when the Prince and Princess of Wales and their daughters, the Princesses Louise, Victoria and Maude, took up their positions behind the bridesmaids. Apart from a handful of loyal servants, gardeners and gamekeepers, there was hardly a guest who did not count among what *Queen* magazine, a 'society' magazine of the day, called 'the top ten thousand'. Among them sat Charles Hoare and his wife Margaret. The gossip columns had not begun to comment on the affair between Charles and Beatie, but gossip about the details of the unusual measures her parents had taken in order to keep the lovers apart would have spread to most of the congregation, who would have watched – discreetly, of course – to see if anything passed between them. There was the added *frisson* from the knowledge that Charles had extended Kelsey Manor in order to entertain the Prince of Wales in becoming style.

In the world outside Berkeley Castle, to which Beatie returned after the wedding, Charles worked hard at building a reputation as the busiest and most extravagant Master the hunt had ever known. He began by moving to Cirencester, where he took over the lease of the house on Cecily Hill recently vacated by his predecessor Lord Shannon. The house stood in a cul-de-sac closed off by elegant wrought-iron gates. Beyond them was a five-mile ride across Cirencester Park, the property of Lord Bathurst. In effect, Charles, the Master of the VWH, was living a stone's throw from the home of the Chairman, whose house was on the edge of the town, screened from it by grey walls and the highest yew hedge in the world. Occasionally, Master and Chairman would start a day's hunting at the most congenial point imaginable – outside Cecily Hill House itself, with the vast acreage of the park, superb hunting country, the other side of the iron gates.

Charles planned to hunt six days a week and, for that purpose, built up three separate packs. In fact he hunted five days with the VWH and went out with the Badminton on Monday, which was market-day in Cirencester, where most of his followers had business.

Whatever his failings, it could not be denied that Charles, now in his early thirties, was a man of immense energy who relished hunting as – in the words of Mr Jorrocks – 'the sport of kings, the image of war without its guilt, and only five-and-twenty per cent of its danger'. The hunting world around Cirencester was light-years away from the decks of the *Mercury*, but, when Charles made the leap from one to the other, he imposed a hardy and strenuous life on the boys in his care with the ease of a man who had known as much himself – and rejoiced in it.

As Charles's fortunes were waxing in Cirencester, those of Arthur Sumner in the neighbouring Cotswold country were waning as the cost of running a hunt club drained his limited resources.

Mrs Hoare, in the meantime, was settling into Cirencester life, untouched as yet by the differing fortunes of the two local Masters of Foxhounds, and unaware that they were to prove major ingredients in the troubles that lay ahead. She busied herself with the social and cultural life of the locality, organizing concerts to raise money for charities.

Beatie, languishing in the seclusion of Berkeley Castle, should have been cut off from the events in Cirencester, but her descendants are not so sure of this. The culprit, they believe, was a close relation, Winifred Ida, who had just married Lord Rocksavage. The latter was twenty-one and his bride seventeen, three months older than Beatie. As a married woman, Winifred could now walk with a 'larger tether', and it is possible that Beatie enlisted her to carry messages in and out of the castle and arrange assignations. Later, she found another ally in Major Fitzhardinge Kingscote, known to his intimates as Fitz.

Fitz was Colonel Kingscote's half-brother. He was born in 1837, and joined the army in 1854. In November of that year, still only seventeen, he was promoted from ensign to lieutenant. It was the time of the Crimean War and the half-brothers were in the campaign, Fitz as a dashing young officer in the thick of the fighting, and Nigel, nearly ten years his senior, on Lord Raglan's staff. Wherever they turned there were reminders of their origins and the lives they led before they were caught up in the war. The literature of the war is huge, with every indication that the whole was run by the tight coterie of the interrelated few whose origins and connections are carefully recorded, if only to assure themselves of their provenance. To the definition of war as 'diplomacy carried on by other means' might be added war as 'social intercourse carried on in dire circumstances'. All the elements of hunting were present: the excitement, the colour, the danger, the opportunities to impress and to be blooded in a way that, should one survive, it would be to add to a prestige that was almost guaranteed merely by being there. The courtly dance, in which the elements of what was or was not gallant and gentlemanly, was played out, but with a hard edge. All too often the expectations of those who deemed themselves born to lead should play the part for real did so with disastrous results.

Which may have been why Fitz collected an injury that nearly killed him. His right hand was smashed in the fighting at the Redan and for the rest of his life he wore a hook where his right hand should have been. He stayed in the army, becoming a captain in 1856, and attaining the rank of major before he retired in 1868. Along the way he served in Canada, India and Ireland. In Canada, he met and married Agnes Grant Stuart, and when he left the army they settled in Ireland, where they had eight children and made a precarious living, renting property in the country and taking in paying guests who came for the hunting. England, however, was still home, and he made frequent visits, staying with relatives in Gloucestershire.

When Charles pressed him into service, Fitz's financial difficulties were becoming acute. In early middle age he was still handsome, though he confessed to his diary that he had his hair tinted bronze. He was a charming, genial man, who had proved himself to be brave almost to the point of madness, and would hunt over the wildest country with his one good hand.

Beatie emerged from Berkeley Castle early in 1881 with those responsible for keeping her there harbouring a strong suspicion that the exercise had been a waste of time. She had had access to horses and was such a superb horsewoman that few could keep up with her if she left the castle for a ride over the Gloucestershire countryside. Short of locking her in her rooms there was really no way in which her guardians could prevent her from making contact with Charles, and in March of that year the eighteen-year-old Beatie conspired to spend over four months in his house on Cecily Hill, sleeping in a room directly over that occupied by his wife. The latter pasted four newspaper cuttings into her leather-bound scrapbook that indicated how this was achieved, and what followed after. The first two describe an incident during a meet of the VWH near Barnsley, a village four miles out of Cirencester on the road to Burford:

> Accident to Miss Sumner. On Tuesday March 1st a somewhat serious accident happened to Miss Sumner, daughter of Captain Sumner, Master of the Cotswold Hounds. The accomplished equestrienne joined a party in the meet of the V.W.H. Hounds at Barnsley. In the course of a hot run she was negotiating a difficult fence – a stone stile with a ditch on the taking off side, when her horse made a mistake, slipped into the grip, and threw the fair rider violently upon her head and shoulders. As quickly as possible a conveyance was procured and the sufferer brought into the residence of Mr. C.A.R. Hoare, where she was attended by a medical gentleman and found not to be seriously injured as was at first supposed. Captain Sumner subsequently arrived and stopped with his daughter for some days.[6]

The second report differs in only one detail saying that 'Captain Sumner subsequently arrived and stayed in the town.'[7]

31

Her descendants are in little doubt as to what really happened on that day. Beatie was not thrown when her horse made a mistake: she deliberately threw herself to the ground. She faked the whole business, with Charles's connivance, so that she could gain a means of entry to his house, and her questionable injury provided the excuse for her stay there.

Chatcomb was the setting for the next act. What took place is summarised in the third of Margaret Hoare's cuttings:

Monday, the 7th. Cotswold at Chatcomb. A big muster, including Captain Sumner and Miss Sumner (who we very much regret to hear she met with an accident while out with the V.W.H. Hounds on Tuesday last, when her horse fell and rolled on her. She was taken at once to Cirencester, where medical assistance was obtained, and I feel assured I only echo the sentiments of all connected with the Hunting in this neighbourhood by saying I sincerely trust she is not seriously hurt and that we shall see her in the saddle again), Mr. C. Hoare . . .[8]

The article continues with another two dozen names of the principal hunt members.

Charles hunted that day, and the teenage Beatie watched from his carriage. She returned – disconcertingly – not to her own home a mere three miles away in Cheltenham, but to her 'sick-bed' in Cecily Hill House, Cirencester, twelve miles in completely the opposite direction.

Almost unchanged since it was built, Cecily Hill House rises up from the pavement, three storeys, double-fronted, its windows set in thick walls, the whole capped by a pediment that gives it a distinctly classical look. Its neighbours on both sides of the road complement its character, ranging from a terrace of houses at the entrance nearest the town, to a mock Norman castle beside the gate leading into Cirencester Park and the five-mile ride. Most were built in the early nineteenth century. At the rear of Cecily Hill House a small garden slopes down to a wall. A door opens onto a footbridge over a fast-flowing stream paralleled by a footpath, the route of servants and tradespeople visiting the house.

The 1881 census tells of an ample household. Charles and Margaret Hoare and three children are waited on by a staff of fourteen, from a butler of sixty-five to a hall boy of sixteen. Four visitors are listed, including three young women, one of them Beatrice H. Sumner, eighteen, whose birthplace is listed incorrectly as London, Middlesex.

In London the occupants of Stafford House, the largest and most palatial privately owned house in the city, responded to the demands of the census. The list began with the Duke and Duchess of Sutherland, the Marquess of Stafford followed by Georgina E.H. Sumner, Beatie's mother. Twenty-seven servants were listed.

In April, a newspaper published the last of the four items about Beatie at the house, bracketed together by Mrs Hoare:

> Miss Sumner is still confined to her bed at Cirencester in consequence of the spinal injury she received at the time of her accident in the hunting field a month ago.[9]

So blatant was the impropriety that Beatie's father could not ignore it and, in July, he approached Charles directly and upbraided him for his dishonourable conduct. Charles admitted it, as did Beatie: there was not much else they could do. They both wept bitterly.[10] It was a touching scene which might have softened the harsher judgements of those outside Cecily Hill House had they been witness to it – the big man of the hunting world and the young girl, helpless in the face of their passion for each other.

Trying to keep Beatie in Berkeley Castle had proved such a failure that the next gambit was to have recourse to the law. On 20 December 1881 Beatie was made a ward of court, her status in law being that of an infant. Injunctions were served on her and Charles restraining them from having 'any intercourse or communication, direct or indirect'.[11] At first they tried rather feebly to obey the injunctions, but in June 1882 there began a series of events that made the court order hardly worth the paper on which it was written.

Beatie's father was in deep financial trouble. He faced bankruptcy, the most galling immediate result of which was the seizure of his horses. The census that recorded his daughter's presence at Cecily Hill House found him living in Rosehaugh Villa, Pittville Circus with two of his children and a mere four servants. It was a substantial house of the kind rented by wealthy visitors to Cheltenham who came to take the waters at the Pittville Pump Room less than half a mile away. It was not an address for people of precarious means. Mrs Sumner, desperate to stave off the disaster, eventually obtained £200 from Lord Rocksavage, the newest member of the family since his marriage to Winifred. When Beatie suggested Charles as a source of funds she upbraided her daughter for her wickedness at putting such temptation before her, but by the following morning she had made up her mind. To save her husband she was going to write to Charles and ask him for a loan of £3,000 – a figure slightly larger than her husband's actual debts. The letter written, she asked Beatie to read it before sending her out to post it. As she explained much later, she could not give it to a servant and she was not going out herself.[12]

Charles's reply came back, offering cash, but only on condition that Mr Sumner was fully informed about what was happening. Mr Sumner, however, was not at home, and had not been for some time. He was staying with Lord Fitzhardinge. Beatie and her mother consulted the family solicitor, a Mr Chesshyre, about the feasibility of borrowing money from the man with whom Beatie was forbidden to communicate and a way was found for the transaction to take place. Mrs Sumner sent for her husband, explained the position, and in due course and with his full approval the money was formally applied for and delivered. Mrs Sumner, who had little notion of how financial transactions were conducted, had originally asked for £3,000 – she wouldn't settle for less – 'cash, in a lump, in an envelope'.[13] The transfer through the office of Mr Chesshyre was less crudely achieved. It did, however, give rise to the story, which persisted for over a hundred years, that Charles had bought Beatie from her parents for the sum of £3,000.

Their financial problems eased, Mrs Sumner at once arranged a tour of Germany with her daughter. Something of her ineffectuality, her tendency to rely on Beatie, is demonstrated by the fact that she asked her daughter to invite Major Kingscote, Beatie's Uncle Fitz, to accompany them, and for the next two years he was almost constantly at hand.

Before they left in mid-July 1882, Beatie persuaded her Uncle Fitz to ask his solicitor, a Mr Inderwick, if it would be possible for two people, kept apart by a court order in England, to meet abroad.[14] The solicitor's reply was unequivocal: yes, two such people could meet, but no, they would never be able to return to England again without answering to the law. The law applied no matter where they went.

Even though the grave consequences of any breach of the court order had been spelled out to him, Fitz took up the task of keeping Charles and Beatie in touch. He was in debt to Charles, from whom he had begun to borrow earlier that year, leaving his carriage as security. He wrote from Weilbad asking for a further loan, and persuaded Beatie to include her letters in the same envelopes as a safeguard against detection. Charles could always say that he had never knowingly received a letter from Beatie for the simple reason that her handwriting never appeared on the envelope.[15]

They returned to London in September, and Fitz took Beatie to the home of her widowed aunt, Mrs Martin, at 20 Seymour Street. Unknown to them, Mrs Martin's butler, James Kennelly, had already begun collecting the kind of evidence that would prove so damaging when the lovers appeared in court in 1885. In July, just before their departure to Germany, Kennelly had answered the door when a cabman came to collect Beatie, declaring that Mr Hoare had sent him. Kennelly took the cabman's number, 8592, and told all in an affidavit in May 1884.[16]

Beatie had presents for Charles – a whip and a stick she had bought in Germany – so her uncle tried to arrange a meeting between them at the Great Western Hotel in Paddington. Fitz took the presents into the hotel, leaving Beatie in the cab, but Charles, mature and discreet, refused to accept them and steeled himself not to see Beatie even when Fitz told him she was crying in the cab outside.[17] On another occasion, Fitz and his niece were on the same train as Charles, but in different compartments. When it stopped at a station, Fitz tried to persuade Charles to come into the same compartment as them, but he ran out of the station leaving Beatie in tears.

In October of the same year, 1882, a second trip abroad began. This time there were four in the party after another uncle, Edgar Hanbury, joined them. They stayed in Paris, visiting the Louvre and Notre Dame, and attending the theatre in the evening. Fitz kept his diary and recorded their stays in Bologna, Florence, Rome and Milan. Their pleasures were unremarkable and consisted of the conventional English tourist round.

After their return to London in November, Beatie moved into 31 Halsey Street, Cadogan Square, where she was in the care of a Madame Mosson, who was employed by Colonel Kingscote specifically for the purpose.

On 12 July 1883, Beatie celebrated her twenty-first birthday by going to the offices of Inderwick with Charles to ask if there was anything in law to prevent them living together. There were no obstacles apart from moral ones, the solicitor assured them.[18]

For six years the two had defied all attempts at separating them. The rules for the upbringing of a young Victorian lady of 'good' family had hardly applied to the defiant, spirited Beatie, who wanted her own way in everything. In fact her singularity can hardly be stressed enough. She had two sisters who went through the careful grooming appropriate to their class and married well – Madelaine to Sir George Banks Jenkinson, and Gertrude to Admiral Heaton-Ellis – but she would have none of it. There was no 'coming out' for her, no presentation at Court in spite of her connections with the monarchy. These were not merely the stuff of genealogy. In September 1876 Arthur Sumner was photographed at a country house in Scotland. In the picture he is one of a group of eleven, all dressed for the outdoors, most of them carrying walking sticks. On Sumner's right stands Albert Edward, Prince of Wales, in front of him Prince George, eleven years old, who will succeed his father as George V, to his left Alexandra, Princess of Wales, and another son, Prince Albert Victor. In this formidable company Sumner is a tall figure, slightly built, with a large nose in a thin, anxious face. Sloping narrow shoulders, a droopy moustache and straggly beard add to a look of frailty.

So extreme was Beatie's attitude that it takes no more than a little amateur psychology to predict that, in the event of her ever relenting, she would be the victim of a sort of psychological inversion. Indiscipline would be intolerable in others when she reflected on the harm it had done to her own life. Sexual phenomena would become distasteful to a woman who had once been ruled by her desires. The sexuality perhaps of her children, certainly of the boys she was eventually to rule, would be crushed by driving them to the point of exhaustion every day of their lives, and by keeping them so hungry that they had no interests but in food, sleep and survival.

For a while after her coming of age Beatie continued to live with Madame Mosson. Her Uncle Fitz returned to his wife and children in Galway, but was back in England on 3 August, when he dined with Beatie and Charles and then accompanied them to the theatre.

The following day they went to stay at the Granville Hotel, Ramsgate, with Uncle Fitz once again in his role as chaperone. Madame Mosson had disappeared on holiday for a few weeks. Fitz was certain that nothing improper took place between his two companions, at least not while they were in Ramsgate. He could not be held responsible for them when they went up to London on 28 September, returning the next day. They felt obliged to explain to him where they had slept – Beatie in the empty house in Halsey Street, and Charles at 37 Fleet Street, the premises of Hoare's Bank.[19] Nonetheless, their first child was born nine months later on 23 June 1884. She was christened Sybil. Sixty-one years later she sat with her mother by the open window of The House and listened to the sounds drifting from the ship in the middle of the River Hamble. Beatie and Charles had a second child on 20 September 1886, Keith Robin.

There seemed little point in concealing their relationship, and the services of Madame Mosson – met off the ferry at Dover at the beginning of October – were swiftly dispensed with. Fitz was sent to Faringdon in Berkshire to look at a shooting box, Wicklesham Lodge, the property of a Colonel Edwards who was abroad on military service. Mr Adams of Faringdon acted as the Colonel's landlord. The house, much extended in recent years, stands on a lonely hilltop site that, in the 1880s, was approached by a long narrow drive that came up almost from Faringdon itself, a mile-and-a-half away. From the house one can see the town and the squat square tower of the parish church near the marketplace. Coincidence can at times astonish, but the modern owner of the lodge who placed a statue of the god Mercury on the lawn outside the southern windows was unaware that this was the first home of Charles and Beatie, the man who founded a school of the same name – and the woman who eventually ran it.

FOUR

The Gloucestershire Scandal

The hunting season of 1883–4 was one of frantic activity on the part of Charles. When it began, Beatie was pregnant and the household at Faringdon was the subject of gossip that found its way into the London weekly papers, with sly references in *Vanity Fair* and *Truth* to 'the uncle . . . who makes an admirable chaperone'. Margaret Hoare diligently cut these out and put them in her scrapbook.[1]

In November, at the start of the season, Lord Fitzhardinge, Colonel Nigel Kingscote and Mr Sumner descended on Inderwick at the solicitor's offices in London, imploring him to put pressure on those at Faringdon to break up a household which they felt was too outrageous to be tolerated.[2] Inderwick tried letters and telegrams without success, addressing them mainly to Fitzhardinge Kingscote, who simply passed them on to Charles. The latter, disenchanted with Inderwick for taking the side of the Kingscote and Sumner families, took his legal problems elsewhere.

The level of Inderwick's desperation comes through in the tone of one of his letters: 'Dear Fitz, For God's sake come and see me. I want to do you a turn if you will only let me.'[3] Charles's wealth was such that he could have retired to any one of half-a-dozen large houses that he either owned or rented, and let the uproar over his relationship with Beatie burn itself out. It would not have been the first time a man of his position had taken such a course, but he seemed compelled to justify his position, to prove to society that he was indifferent to its opinions. To continue in public life meant continuing in the role of Master of the VWH and he did not need to be very clever to see that, for social reasons, the club would sooner or later decide that he would have to go. He had, as it were, carried off a daughter of one of the best connected families in Gloucestershire, one who was welcome in all the great houses – Badminton, Cirencester Park, Berkeley Castle and many more – as a respected relative of the people there. Lord Bathurst, the Chairman of the VWH, had made his position plain early in the season. Arthur Sumner approached him and complained about the ménage at Faringdon of Charles, Beatie and her Uncle Fitz, but was so deeply compromised by his indebtedness to Charles that his words carried no weight. Lord Bathurst wrote to Charles asking for his version of events, and received assurances that the rumours circulating in the country were utterly false. Charles even called on Lord Bathurst to reinforce his story, but the earl would not accept it, saying that 'we must be on different terms from those on which we have hitherto met'.[4]

Charles found his supporters among the tenant farmers. They were in the middle of an agricultural depression as farm prices touched rock bottom in the face of cheap grain imported from the newly opened prairies of North America. Many were reduced to subsistence living, and, when they abandoned their farms, the landlords in turn felt the pinch, as they could not find new tenants. In Charles, the tenant farmers felt that they had found a champion who was rich and was on their side, opposed to the landlords. He plied them with money, food, entertainment, horses, loans, gifts of all kinds but, above all, with sport – hunting conducted with vigour and on a scale unheard of in the entire history of the VWH country. Charles almost lived in the saddle. That season he hunted his hounds on 144 days, killed 82 brace, and ran 15 brace of foxes to ground,[5] a level of sport which made people indulgent towards the man who made it possible, conveniently obscuring for many the details of his personal life.

In spite of the sport he offered, it became clear to Charles that the hunt would soon be split between his supporters and those surrounding Lord Bathurst, and he began laying his plans against that day. He set up a railway service on one day a week that would take horses, hounds and servants from Cirencester to Swindon. Any members who wished to do so could take the train and be in Swindon before lunch, have a good afternoon out, and catch another train back in time for dinner. In his obituary Charles was described as 'opening the Swindon country',[6] as if the Master had set about doing the hunting world a particular favour by bringing the sport to an area where it had previously been lacking. There was no altruism in this bit of organisation. Rather it served to create a stronghold for Charles, an area in which tenant farmers through their sheer numbers would keep him in the field if there were demands for his resignation. The agricultural depression once again served his purpose, enabling him to reinforce his grip on the country by renting huge blocks of land, ostensibly for the shooting, but in fact in order to limit the operations of a rival pack.

During this time Mrs Hoare put a brave face on things and appeared in public with her husband, often arriving in her carriage to see the hunt assemble at the start of a day in the field.[7] But behind the scenes things were beginning to crack. Fitzhardinge Kingscote was getting letters from his half-brother Nigel, telling him of the Kingscote family's disgust at his behaviour. Fitz, however, was so dependent on allowances from Charles that he could not break out of the trap that Wicklesham had become for him. At last he wrote to Inderwick, begging to be released. His letter addressed and dated Faringdon, 3 January 1884, reads:

Dear Mr. Inderwick,
I am willing at once to change my way of life and go to Galway and remain there and estrange myself altogether from my present companions if you can get me the sum of £100 to pay the debts I have contracted in the last few months since I had no regular allowance – also if you are paid what you expended for me and I am guaranteed my fixed regular monthly allowance – If these three things can be arranged I can at once break up this establishment and leave England and end the Scandal.
Yrs, sincerely
F. Kingscote[8]

Fitz, of course, was mistaken in thinking that 'the Scandal' was rooted in his presence at Wicklesham and that his departure would end it. Eventually he left, but when he reached Galway he found that his wife had been kept informed of the situation in England, and in less than two years this handsome woman, still in her early forties, had aged dramatically, her dark hair turned to white.

Back in VWH country, the fight between landlords and tenantry – for that is what it had become – grew more intense. When men on the landowners' side refused to speak to him at a meet, Charles threatened to take the hounds back to kennels, and when, as expected, a call for his resignation was made, his admirers gathered 600 signatures purporting to be those of the tenant farmers who were on his side. The signatures were appended to what was described as a 'memorial', which was little more than a veiled threat, demanding the withdrawal of the request for Charles's resignation. They won their point but the victory was to be short-lived. As early as March 1884 Charles was warned of an action being prepared against him for contempt of court for having, in breach of the court order of December 1881, 'had communication . . . with Beatrice Holme Sumner'.[9]

The action gained momentum in May when, on the 14th, Fitzhardinge Kingscote was traced to Glenina in Co. Galway and persuaded to make an affidavit in which he gave details of nearly two years he had spent with Beatie and Charles.[10] A fortnight later solicitors interviewed James Kennelly,[11] the butler at 20 Seymour Street, and Robert Blott, formerly a servant at the Norfolk Square Hotel, but by this time one of the crew of the *Prins Hendrik*,[12] a steamship trading between London and ports in mainland Europe. Kennelly obligingly told them about the cabman, and Blott about his duties in the hotel rooms Charles had occupied at weekends earlier that year when a lady visited him called Miss Hoare. He was shown photos of Beatie and identified her as the lady.

Charles was sufficiently alarmed by all this to file his own affidavit on 5 June, eleven pages and twenty-seven paragraphs, in which he tried to anticipate all the charges likely to be made against him.[13] Fitzhardinge Kingscote was blamed for persistently trying to get him to communicate with Beatie, and it was revealed that Charles had loaned him £750; nothing was said about his loan of £3,000 to the Sumners. Wicklesham Lodge was not referred to except in such a way as to make Inderwick's desperate efforts to bring to an end the arrangements there in November of the previous year appear impertinent.

Now more than ever Charles needed friends. The Hoare family had left Cecily Hill House and moved to the Querns, an equally spacious place further away from Lord Bathurst's house but still convenient to the kennels; and on 13 August, two months after Sybil's birth, the annual hunt puppy show was held there.[14] Hunt members were there to watch the judging of the puppies at the kennels. These were the animals born the previous year that had been farmed out to 'puppy walkers', people who would look after them from the time they were weaned until they were old and robust enough to be introduced to the pack. As always on these occasions, there was lunch for everybody, Charles paying for food and wine served in a marquee that had been erected in the grounds of the Querns. Margaret dutifully supervised the catering and lunched with the company. With the other ladies present she withdrew when the time came for toasts and speeches.

Charles took the chair. He got to his feet and began a long, rambling and sycophantic speech to an audience composed largely of tenant farmers. He began with a toast to the Queen, and said he was anxious to get through the official and customary toasts, which it was one's duty as well as one's pleasure to propose, as quickly as he could.

Further toasts followed: to the Prince of Wales (who had once hunted with the Cirencester pack), to the Church – not usually responded to at such events, but on this occasion redeemed by the presence in the audience of a clergyman – to the judges, the hunt servants and so forth. There was one striking omission. The Master announced that he would like to drink the health of Earl Bathurst but added, pointedly, that a toast afforded little amusement if there was no one there to respond.

The tenant farmers winked at each other in anticipation of the final toast; he had to propose it, though he dared say he might get into hot water over it. He would be the most ungrateful man in all England if he did not do so and drink heartily, almost to excess, to the tenant farmers and others of this country (cheers). Why it had not come first on the list was that he feared it might appear selfish on his part if he did so. It was a toast which he felt very much bound up in, for a good many things had occurred which proved to him how extremely tight was the knot which was tied between him and the country, evidenced by the support which had always been extended to him by the tenant farmers (loud cheers). He would not make a long speech to them, it was not his design to set class against class but merely to show by a few wretched miserable words of his how grateful he was to the tenant farmers and others who had met him there, and were not afraid or ashamed to put their names on paper and say, 'That is a man we like' (loud cheering). They had acted unflinchingly, and he thanked the tenant farmers and others most extremely for the way they had stuck to him, and he could only say that as long as ever he could do so he should stick to them (loud cheers).

There followed a great deal more in the same vein. Margaret Hoare, had she been listening, would have heard her husband portray himself as a simple man in language barely above that of a simpleton.

Somebody proposed the health of Mrs Hoare and the ladies who had adorned their table that day. Charles responded, saying that 'there was no man in this world whose duty it was more to thank them for drinking Mrs. Hoare's health'. He said he would not make a long speech, but would simply say one word which comprehended it all; she was 'a woman of a thousand' (loud cheers).[15] His stock rose enormously in the county after this. It declined somewhat when, seven months later, he attended the Court of Chancery in London and heard proclaimed 'a motion on behalf of Colonel Kingscote for the committal to prison of Charles Arthur Richard Hoare for contempt in having disobeyed an injunction of the Court, dated December 20 1881, restraining him from having any intercourse, or communication, directly or indirectly, with Miss Beatrice Holme Sumner, who was then an infant, but attained her full age on July 12th 1883, and also forbidding Miss Sumner to have any intercourse or communication with Mr. Hoare'.[16]

FIVE

The Judgement

On 17 March 1885, Charles and Beatie came to the Court of Chancery in London to hear their eight-year-long affair publicly unravelled. The prospect of scandal in high places was enough to ensure the major newspapers – from *The Times* to the *News of the World* – would be there, avid for details. The best counsel were on hand, twelve altogether, to represent the different parties. Seven were QCs, including the Attorney General, Sir Henry James. On the bench was Mr Justice Chitty.[1]

Before them were the affidavits of the people involved. Beatie's ran to eleven substantial pages.[2] The clerk who penned her words, innocent of the difference between some aristocratic names as spelled and spoken, wrote what he heard and put 'Chumney' for 'Cholmondeley'. Nobody thought to correct him. Some of its paragraphs were reported verbatim in *The Times* and in the Gloucestershire papers. The £3,000 loan, including Beatie's mother's request for 'cash, in a lump, in an envelope', was described. She elaborated on the trips abroad. Of her uncle's involvement she said that 'my mother told me to ask my Uncle, Major Fitzhardinge Kingscote, to accompany us on the plea that he would be a companion to me and that it would be beneficial to him to get him out of England as he was behaving in a disgraceful way'.[3] She implicated the Major, her cousin, Winifred Ida, now the Marchioness of Cholmondeley, and her cousin's husband in the business of communicating with Charles.

The affidavit of the Marchioness, whose husband had acceded to the title of Marquess the previous year, told an entirely different story of having struggled to show Beatie the error of her ways and

46

keep her away from Charles.[4] There was an affidavit from Inderwick,[5] protesting that Charles had interfered with a key witness, the cab driver who had called at the house in Seymour Street to collect Beatie. The cabbie, Thomas Aldous, had been due at Inderwick's office one Sunday, promising to give a good deal of incriminating evidence about Charles and Beatie, and when he failed to arrive there was a strong suspicion that Charles had bribed him not to attend.

Colonel Nigel Kingscote, who had brought the case to court, was only marginally less damaging than Beatie in his revelations of what had happened while his niece had been a ward of court and thereafter. He touched on the arrangements at Wicklesham Lodge, Faringdon, and remarked on 'the considerable scandal created in the Hunting field by the conspicuous attentions of Mr. Hoare to the Plaintiff'.[6]

The most strikingly worded document was that submitted by Arthur Randall Huitt, 'Gentleman and Solicitor of the High Court of Justice', in which he stated that:

> On the ninth day of March 1885, I served the Right Honourable the Marquess of Cholmondeley and the Right Honourable the Marchioness of Cholmondeley of Higginsfield in the County of Chester with a notice in writing instituted in this Action addressed respectively to the said Marquess of Cholmondeley and Marchioness of Cholmondeley and purporting to be a Notice of Motion to be made to Mr. Justice Chitty herein for the committal to Prison of them the said Marquess of Cholmondeley and Marchioness of Cholmondeley by delivering a true copy of the said notice . . .[7]

It may have been a mere form of words in which the court asserted its authority over those who were among the highest in the land as much as over the humblest cab driver or hotel servant involved in the case, but they were words that were to come perilously close to being enacted.

All but one of the protagonists were in court.[8] The Marquess and Marchioness sat in fear of what the day might hold for them. Mr and Mrs Sumner steeled themselves against the moment when their weakness in the face of their daughter's excesses would be revealed. The Earl Bathurst was there in response to a subpoena summoning him to appear as a witness in the case. Nearby was a small band of witnesses from London – a housekeeper, a cabman, the butler from Seymour Street, and hotel servants, among them Robert Blott, who would have things to say which would help plot the twists and turns of an extraordinary affair. Colonel Nigel Kingscote was present – a man who had spent over forty years in the Royal Household as Groom-in-Waiting to Queen Victoria and later as Equerry to the Prince of Wales. Only the Colonel's half-brother, Uncle Fitz, was missing. He was said to be untraceable, presumably having gone to Ireland to be well out of the way, for he knew that his presence there would be disastrous to many people. Sadly, in his absence there is every indication that he was used as a scapegoat, someone who could be vilified freely since he was in no position to defend himself.

The proceedings opened with Mr Ince QC, in support of the motion, saying that Colonel Kingscote's position was simply that of a trustee in whom a fund had been invested for the purpose of protecting Miss Sumner, and that he felt it to be his duty to bring forward the facts of the case and leave the matter in the hands of the court. In a caustic aside, he said that Mr Hoare had begun his attentions to Beatie 'when she was barely out of the cradle'.

Mr Charles Russell QC, on behalf of Miss Sumner, objected to the motion being opened at all. Miss Sumner was now twenty-three years of age. She was in fact no party to the motion, and she disclaimed proceedings that could no longer be said to be taken for her protection or in her interest, but rather to be actuated by private motives. On her behalf he protested emphatically against proceedings that could only be prejudicial to her interests.

When Charles's counsel, Mr Davey QC, got to his feet, the court might have expected an opening shot along the same formal lines as those used by Ince and Russell, protesting his client's innocence, perhaps, or at least reaffirming, the point already made – that Beatie was no longer a ward of court, and that the motives of Colonel Kingscote in bringing the case were questionable. He began, however, by objecting to the reading of affidavits that, he said, contained merely hearsay evidence; no evidence could be admitted except that which was within the strictest rules of admissibility.

When Mr Ince rose to announce that he would read Major Kingscote's affidavit, Davey was on his feet again, protesting loudly. He knew that if Charles Hoare was going to end up in prison this was the document that would see it effected.

'Is Major Kingscote here to be cross-examined?' asked Davey.

'You know well enough why he is not here,' said Ince, piqued at this reminder that the one witness who could help his client's case could not be found.

Mr Justice Chitty said he would hear the affidavit, adding wearily, 'I fail to see the value of this fencing'.

Still on the defensive, Davey objected in advance to any evidence that was not to do with the period under discussion – the eighteen months during which Beatie was a ward of court. He knew only too well what was coming: not just the details of the irregularities during that period, the lovers constantly in touch through the busy offices of Fitz and the then Lady Rocksavage, but the aftermath, the rush to seek assurances from Inderwick that the law could not touch them if they decided to live together openly. There would be the matter of Beatie's pregnancy, and the household at Faringdon would be mentioned along with the other addresses she had stayed at – Halsey Street, Seymour Street, and another in St John's Wood. All this on top of earlier extravagances, trips to the Continent and an opulent life in London of theatres and dining out, would destroy his client. At some point the question 'Who had paid for all this?' would be asked. Not bankrupt Mr Sumner, that was certain, nor Fitz Kingscote with his tenuous grip on solvency, nor Colonel Kingscote with his 'fund invested for the purpose of protecting Miss Sumner'. It had to be Charles Hoare, senior partner in the bank of the same name. For Davey there loomed the prospect of his client going to prison, with the risk that those who had abetted him would go too. Charles, Beatie, her cousin Lady Cholmondeley, Fitz Kingscote and Mr and Mrs Sumner stood in a row like dominoes; if one fell the whole lot would go, and what had been a minor provincial scandal would explode beyond the bounds of Chancery into the Court of Queen Victoria, with two of Her Majesty's closest and most trusted servants, the Marquess of Cholmondeley and Colonel Kingscote, embarrassed by the public humiliation of erring relatives.

Major Fitz Kingscote's affidavit was read, but it was not until Mr Justice Chitty delivered his judgement that Davey learned with relief that only those parts were admissible which witnesses present in the court had corroborated.

The bit players took the stage. A servant who had seen Beatie and Charles at the Great Western Hotel identified them when they were ordered to stand up for his inspection. Robert Blott – fetched off his ship to give evidence – answered questions about meetings in the Norfolk Square Hotel. Thomas Aldous, the cab driver who had been spotted by James Kennelly at Seymour Street, provided a little light relief. He began by demanding his expenses since his cab was being kept waiting (laughter). He said he never was in the service of Lord Cholmondeley. Lord Cholmondeley was formerly Rocksavage. His (Thomas Aldous's) acquaintance lay among noblemen (laughter). It did not include Mr Hoare (more laughter). He knew Miss Sumner. In 1883 he saw her in Sloane Street, and afterwards she gave him orders to drive her. He used to give that lady his account, and she used to pay him. He very seldom drove Miss Sumner alone. She was usually accompanied by one of her own sex. She was sometimes accompanied by a gentleman.

One by one the stratagems Charles and Beatie had used in order to communicate with each other were exposed. The court learned of the extraordinary lengths Colonel Kingscote and Mr Sumner had gone to, to keep them apart, including the period in which they tried to confine Beatie to Berkeley Castle under the eyes of Lord and Lady

Fitzhardinge. The 'accident in the hunting field', which led to four months of the lovers under the same roof while Beatie was still in her teens, was described in detail. One can only guess at the bewilderment of those in court when it transpired that these people, who had striven so diligently to keep the banker and the girl apart, had gone on to borrow money from the one at the suggestion of the other.

Mr Ince cross-examined Charles who had, predictably, to answer questions about the possibility of his having funded the eighteen months of high life enjoyed by Beatie, her mother and uncle. It was a dangerous moment, and would have been more dangerous still had Uncle Fitz been present. As it was, Charles was able to imply that the £3,000 he loaned to Mr Sumner may have been used for purposes other than that of paying debts. Ince did not give up, but accused Charles of selling horses to Lord Rocksavage and of adding to the price an amount that was then passed on to Beatie. Charles denied this, and Ince did not pursue the point.

A sad moment in the proceedings occurred when Beatie's cousin the Marchioness of Cholmondeley, formerly Lady Rocksavage, entered the witness box. The grand titles weighed heavily on this spirited young woman of high intelligence and great good humour who went on to a distinguished career of public service. Until that moment it had all been a great lark for her, an exciting diversion for someone whose social condition provided few outlets for her capabilities. When the case was over, a London correspondent was moved to write to the *Gloucestershire Chronicle*:

In exculpation of the conduct of Lady Cholmondeley, which has filled everybody with surprise, one fact should be stated – at the time when she acted so imprudently she was only 17 years of age. Engaged at 16, and married at 17, with apparently no experience of life and still a mere girl, she probably acted in mere thoughtlessness, and with no such intention as has been attributed to her in quarters where a kindlier judgement would have been accorded her had her age been known.

No one was moved to write in exculpation of the conduct of the tough-minded Beatie who was only fifteen years of age when she began her affair with Charles. The first day's proceedings ended with the court hearing how Fitz Kingscote had accompanied Beatie, her mother and her Uncle Edgar on the trip to Rome in 1882.

When the case was resumed the following day, Mr Davey was still in the business of limiting the damage to his client, Charles Hoare, since much of the evidence heard by then was so damning, particularly that concerning events after Beatie had come of age. He was at pains to tell the court what it already knew, that the effect of the order making Beatie a ward of court ceased when she came of age, and that the court 'could not make an order restraining two adult persons from holding communication with each other'. He turned next to the subject of the letters sent by Beatie to Charles, a subject vital to the case, since it was the strongest evidence there was that they had disobeyed the injunction served on each of them – that they should not communicate in any way whatsoever while one of them was, in the eyes of the law, an infant. That one party, the lady in the case, had dispatched letters, and that the other had received them, was indisputable. Davey's defence – a stratagem planned, as we have seen, some time before – was that the recipient did not know from whom they came since the sender's handwriting did not appear on the envelope.

Mr. Justice Chitty:
If Mr. Hoare had sent the letters to the father or to the Court he would have relieved himself of responsibility. That is the strict rule.

Mr. Davey:
Mr. Hoare would have not had the feeling of a man if he had sent the letters to the Court. Some men would rather die than do such a thing.

Mr. Justice Chitty:
Some men would sooner die than keep the law, no doubt. But in all this Mr. Hoare's mature age and the fact that he was a married man has to be remembered.

From letters, Davey quickly turned to affidavits, particularly that from Major Fitz Kingscote. The chief evidence against Mr Hoare, he argued, was contained in this affidavit from a witness whom, of all others, it would have been expedient to have examined. Once again he asked His Lordship to attach no weight to his evidence except insofar as it was corroborated. What Davey forbore to mention was that Fitz in court would have been harder to discredit than the piece of paper he sent in his stead.

There were a few more exchanges before Mr Justice Chitty delivered his judgement, the most telling of which came from Mr Ince when he described Beatie as 'having suffered a fall from which no woman could live to recover'. Like everybody else present, except Charles, he underrated the woman. None was moved to describe him as a 'fallen man'.

The committal proceedings in this Court of Chancery were highly peculiar. They were not criminal proceedings, but public civil proceedings to enforce a penal process against a public offender. There was no jury, and the judge would decide both fact and law – that is, what had taken place, and what decision should be handed down on the strength of this. He would answer, in effect, yea or nay to 'the motion on behalf of Colonel Kingscote for the committal to prison of Charles Arthur Richard Hoare for contempt in having disobeyed an injunction of the Court'.

Mr Justice Chitty delivered his judgement with a long preamble that summarised in brilliant detail the entire proceedings. Then one by one he spelled out the points at which the people before him were 'found to be in breach of the Court order'. They were left in no doubt that he was in a position to commit them. 'Lady Cholmondeley', he said, 'undoubtedly committed a breach of the order, and ladies must know, in whatever situation of life they may be, that orders of the Court are not mere pieces of paper binding men only, but that they bind ladies equally.'

However, all was not yet lost. Several things saved Charles from a prison sentence, and those who stood fearfully in his shadow awaiting the outcome. The first was the absence of Major

Fitzhardinge Kingscote. The second was the latter's affidavit, which was so revealing in its account of Beatie's behaviour that, as Justice Chitty chose to put it, 'one could not take the word of a man who would so dishonour his own niece'. The items of evidence which served most in keeping Charles from prison, however, were those which told of his efforts to obey the court order in the face of temptations to do otherwise, notably on the day Beatie was brought to his hotel with presents she had bought for him in Germany.

The case was closed with the following words from the bench: 'Putting all the circumstances together I think, although I can make an order to commit him [Charles Hoare] I shall do sufficient justice in this case if I order him, as I can do, to pay the costs.'[9]

The newspapers of the day reported the case in great detail, *The Times* and the *News of the World* giving them especial prominence. To the modern reader, they seem – rather like accounts of the Wilde trial – remarkably decorous. There was no attempt to get dramatic mileage out of the appearance in court of so many highly placed men and women, with all their titles and powerful connections, no descriptions, in the absence of photographs, of their attire, nothing about the way in which they conducted themselves. The weekly papers *Truth* and *Vanity Fair* did, however, have some sharp things to say about what had taken place. In the edition of *Truth* dated 26 March 1885 the editor wrote: 'I cannot conceive in whose interest the suit against Mr. Hoare was brought. The evil had already been done, and it assuredly was not remedied by washing dirty linen in public. Was Miss Sumner the gainer, or did her parents and relatives who improved the occasion by borrowing money of Mr. Hoare, profit by this public exposure?'[10] The editor of Vanity Fair castigated Colonel Kingscote for taking so long to bring his case to court, and went on to say that: 'His grounds, as it turns out, were wholly insufficient, and even had they been sufficient it seems very ill judged on his part to have made an attempt necessarily involving sad disclosures relative to his own family, without the possibility of doing any good whatever, either to them or to the young lady.'[11]

Neither *Truth* nor *Vanity Fair*, nor in fact any of the papers, remarked on the strength of feeling that lay behind this extraordinary business. Nobody noted that the Colonel, in his determination to bring Charles Hoare to account for his behaviour, had put at risk his own daughter, the Marchioness of Cholmondeley. This reflected the outrage felt in Gloucestershire by a group of people who had watched in disbelief as a man, ostensibly of their own social class, had exposed them to ridicule.

If they had hoped – and it was a reasonable hope given the amount of 'dirty linen' exposed to public view – that the cause of all their troubles would now quietly withdraw from the scene, they were mistaken. Charles returned to the attack in Gloucestershire, and the storm continued. Beatie went with him. She probably had no choice; the great houses where she had once been a welcome guest were now closed to her. Her parents, brutally shamed by the whole business, fled the country. They went to Malta, never to return. Arthur Sumner died there in 1895, and his wife moved to Switzerland, where she survived him a further twelve years. Margaret Hoare was now totally alienated from her husband, but steadfastly refused to divorce him. The legacy of suffering and bitterness was to affect her family and their descendants well into the twentieth century. Cheerful, bluff, amiable Uncle Fitz, who had strayed into the affair with the first invitation to travel in Europe, and had become so deeply enmeshed that he had to write the pitiful letter to Inderwick in order to disentangle himself, had his marriage brought almost to the point of destruction. Only the compassion and understanding of his tough Canadian wife, whom her husband's aristocratic relatives despised as a 'colonial', saved it from ruin.

Colonel Kingscote, who brought the case to court, did not escape unscathed. After the mauling he received in the gossip magazines he began to withdraw from public life, beginning by resigning as Member of Parliament for Gloucester. He continued to hold responsible posts at Court, however, but these were not in the public eye. Although his efforts were rewarded with a knighthood, his family went into decline after his death. For centuries English monarchs had never been without Kingscotes as soldiers – there was a Kingscote at Agincourt – equerries and ladies-in-waiting, dutiful and utterly reliable, the very backbone of the monarchy itself. After the First World War the heir to the Kingscote estate was killed in a car crash. The land was sold off and the house eventually pulled down. The only memorials to those centuries of service are the tablets on the inner walls of Kingscote village church and the family vault outside, an underground chamber a few yards from the church's eastern extremity. Beatie's mother is close by, brought home from Switzerland for burial at the heart of the village where she was born. A small angelic figure surmounts the grave, wings swept back, her left hand holding a cross with its shaft lying in the fold of her arm, her right hand raising aloft a laurel wreath. Her head is up, her hair blown back from a triumphant face. The figure stands on the forepart of a ship. There is a poignant inscription that speaks of the 'unforgettable love' for her of Madelaine Jenkinson, Beatie's sister, words that probably hide the desolation of one whose last semblance of family life was shattered with the departure of her parents to exile in Malta.

So great was the mayhem in the wake of the 'Gloucestershire Scandal', as it came to be called in the newspapers, that even the philanthropic gesture which Charles made in apparent expiation for what he had done – founding the *Mercury* – seemed empty. The cynical saw it as a cover for his continued relationship with Beatie, who could appear at the school as a housekeeper or matron.

In his judgement Mr Justice Chitty had remarked on 'the cumbersome manner in which Mr. Hoare gave his evidence'. It was the only aside in all that was said and written about the case that revealed something of the bearing of the man at the centre of it. Cumbersome was an understatement; he was crushingly insensitive, bullying those people he could not buy. It was evident that he had reached mature years without reaching maturity. Neither the fields of Devon nor the 'university of the world' had brought him the disciplines that lead to freedom and the ability to choose sensibly among the many alternatives that life offers. A lifetime of self-indulgence, fuelled by his enormous income from the family banking business, had left him without the strategies to cope with the girl of fire and character he had met out riding to hounds. He must, however, have begun to realise that in Beatie Sumner he had stumbled on an original, a one-off, uneducated like himself, but with a rough genius buried somewhere in her psyche which his means might serve to release.

They left the court together, Charles with his meagre absolution and lighter in pocket by a small fortune in legal fees. Later that year he would found his new school, the *Mercury*, not knowing that it was to become his refuge, the source of his transformation into a totally different kind of man, and the basis of an astonishing career for the woman he loved.

SIX

Binstead Hard

After the court case Charles wasted time, money and effort that could have gone into setting up the *Mercury*, fighting tenaciously to retain some elements of the only way of life he knew. The fight began in Cirencester.

In April a meeting of subscribers, members and owners of coverts in the VWH Hunt was held at the King's Head Hotel, convened, as it was delicately put, 'by circular issued by the Hunt Secretary, Mr. Edward Trinder, rendered necessary by the serious differences of opinion existing on the question of the retention of the Mastership by Mr. C.A.R. Hoare'.[1]

About a hundred men gathered in one of the public rooms of the hotel, those supporting Charles slightly outnumbering those against him. While it was one of those occasions from which women were excluded it was also one that they might have preferred to miss. The air was thick with tobacco smoke and with the rather too hearty greetings of tenant farmers as they covered their nervousness at finding themselves in conflict with powerful figures who might remember their temerity at some future date when rents and tenure came up for review. Earl Bathurst was in the chair, and at his side were the Earl of Suffolk and Berkshire, Sir Michael Hicks-Beach MP, and Mr W. Cripps. Nearby were other landowners, some of them the ancestors of people who own and farm the same land today.

To Lord Bathurst fell the duty of spelling out the business of the meeting, put more bluntly this time: the demand for the resignation of Charles Hoare as Master of the VWH. He spoke of years of 'unpleasant gossip and unpleasant reports pervading the country'.

On mentioning the man at the centre of it, he added, 'I observe he is present, and therefore anything I say of course he can contradict.'

It was a long speech, suggesting the dismay of a man, for long comfortable in his wealth and power, who felt unexpectedly threatened. The listeners heard how Charles, who was in any case no longer on speaking terms with Lord Bathurst, had sent a letter to another member of the hunt who had shunned him in similar fashion, saying he would take the hounds back to kennels if that member appeared in the field again. Charles had sent a copy of the letter to Lord Bathurst, but then, as the Earl dryly put it, 'kindly made an exception in my case'. Referring to the trial and his presence there, he went on, 'I was not called on, but I confess it was with considerable surprise that I heard facts admitted which I had been solemnly assured were absolutely false.'

When Lord Suffolk spoke it was to remind the company that a year previously people had signed a petition, or 'memorial', asking that Charles be allowed to continue as Master. He told how, just as the deputation was about to leave the room, one of them had said he would like to know what Charles had done. Now they all knew, and the man had to go.

There were more speeches in the same vein, Sir Michael following Lord Suffolk, then Mr Cripps. All of them attacked Charles; but soon others would have their say, and their cue came from a man who professed his neutrality, who said that he came before them as a stranger, but one who had been devoted to fox-hunting all his life. Reginald Herbert had spent his honeymoon at Kelsey, 'the charming and picturesque seat of Mr. C.A.R. Hoare', and he implied what the majority were waiting to hear – that a new Master would not be allowed to ride over the country, so strong was the feeling on 'the other side', meaning the tenant farmers. There were loud cheers at this, and cries of 'Hear, hear'. Gradually the farmers gained confidence and spoke up for Charles.

One did, however, have the courage to speak against him. Charles was immediately on his feet, launching into a speech that was as bullying as that at the hunt puppy show had been sycophantic.

'Let 'em have it!' shouted a supporter as he got into his stride. He catalogued all he had done for the country, and was cheered all the way. Referring to the scandal he said, 'It seems that but for this moral technicality you would have nothing to say against me.'

He sat down to applause, and remained quiet while the meeting discussed the possibility of canvassing the membership to see if the same support would be found for his continuance in office as in the previous year. Mr Flux, a landowner, brought the company back to the scandal again.

'It has been published everywhere', Flux said.

It is in the face of the world that the gentleman in question himself went into the witness box and was examined by his own counsel – the ablest men of the day – and that no one is able to clear that gentleman of one particle of the soil with which he dirtied himself in the witness box.

Flux went on:

He admitted it – the father of a family which lives before us Cirencester people had to admit himself the father of another child by a young lady, whose name need not be mentioned, with whom he was living. He admitted the occasion for the injunction and that as long as the injunction prevailed and there was peril . . .

Charles exploded. 'The meeting has nothing to do with this!

His men roared their support. When the cheering stopped, Flux lamely tried to resume his speech, but was shouted down. There were a few more speeches before the meeting broke up, including one from a farmer who tried vainly to bring the opposing factions together. But there was to be no reconciliation that evening, and the meeting ended with nothing resolved beyond a decision to canvass the whole membership to see if Charles had as many supporters as before. When this was done a few weeks later, and it was found that he had enough people on his side to make it possible, he split the hunt, setting up his own quarters in Cricklade, a small, exquisite and ancient town eight miles from Swindon on the road to Cirencester, so that by the following year there were two VWH hunt clubs, the Cricklade under Charles Hoare and the Cirencester under Lord Bathurst.

The division was to last for over eighty years, by which time enough generations of huntsmen and women had come and gone for the whole unruly business to have been forgotten, and the membership united again.

The summer of 1885 was spent converting his yacht, the 70-ton *Cyclone*, for use as the training ship he had in mind, and a handful of boys did indeed live on board. When, in later years, people asked among themselves why Charles began this enterprise there were no firm answers to be had. There was, of course, the precedent of his yacht at Exmouth being used to train boys for the sea during the time he lived at Luscombe Castle. Some saw the school as a gesture designed to win back the respect he had enjoyed before his affair with Beatie went public. Though refusing a divorce, Margaret Hoare had left him, taking his sons and their daughter Agatha with her. In her place he had a woman of enormous energy – even in her eighties she could work a sixteen-hour day – for which he had to provide an outlet. The hunting fields of Gloucestershire, and probably of the whole British Isles, were now barred to her. The ship would give her an outdoor life and things to do, but it must have seemed a forlorn hope that she would adapt to a world so different from that she had known.

Not satisfied with the *Cyclone*, Charles searched the London docks for a larger vessel and found the barque *Illovo*, named after a river in South Africa. He bought her and re-named her *Mercury*. She had been built in Aberdeen by H. Hall & Company for Thomas Rennie and her first master, Alexander Airth. She was quite small, approximately 400 gross tons, only 139 feet long, with a width – her 'beam' in nautical language – of 27 feet. She had begun life as a ship-rigged vessel, but her rig had been changed and by 1880 she was recorded in Lloyd's list as a barque. By comparison the *Cutty Sark* in her dry dock in Greenwich, perhaps the most famous merchant sailing ship ever built, is 963 gross tons, with an overall length of 280 feet and a beam of 36 feet. The small dimensions of the *Illovo* had enabled her to cross the sand bars on the African coast and to trade with places inaccessible to most sea-going ships of the time. Small though she was, she was a big step up from the *Cyclone*.[2]

Charles converted the ship into a replica of an early nineteenth-century warship. The hatches were removed and replaced with gratings that let in light and air to the 'tween deck immediately below. The 'tween deck was fitted out with tables and mess fittings so like those of a man-o'-war that one expected to see a cannon in between each table in the manner of HMS *Victory*. Weather-proofed stowage was provided on the main deck for hammocks, again in the style of a fighting ship under sail, where the sailors' bedding gave them protection from enemy gunfire. Mooring booms hung from the sides – long timbers, like sections of masts, which could be swung out at right angles to the ship, reaching out over the water to provide access in all weathers.

Charles bought the topsail schooner *Diana*, 41 tons, as a tender to the ship, and in summer months twenty-five boys at a time used the schooner for cruises in the Channel. He bought small boats for instruction in sailing and rowing, and even a steam launch, in which boys learned the rudiments of engineering. The *Cyclone* went to his wife for whom he provided handsomely.

A staff of fifteen was recruited to administer the ship and instruct the boys, made up of two ex-naval officers and thirteen Able Seaman pensioners. The first boys to be trained were said to be 'improved street arabs of fourteen or fifteen years of age who have vouched for themselves that they are willing to enter the Royal Navy'. They were picked up from the slums of London and quarantined at a cottage in Tooting before being sent to the ship. There, as an Isle of Wight paper put it, they would be 'saved from temporal and eternal ruin'.[3] In a gesture totally out of character with the age and the divisions of society at large, Charles and Beatie took new boys into their own home for a few days before integrating them with the rest of the ship's company.

In his own account of the venture Charles spoke of having created the opportunity for boys of good character from poor families to train for careers at sea. Apart from the HMS *Conway* and HMS *Worcester*, listed as officer cadet ships, he dismissed the twenty other pre-sea schools as reformatories, punishment ships for juvenile offenders. A boy from the lower classes, he maintained, had to commit a crime in order to get pre-sea training, and he was going to change that. In fact there were only three reformatory ships: *Akbar* and *Clarence* on the Mersey and *Cornwall* on the Thames. Eleven industrial training ships, based on the hulks of warships left over from the Napoleonic wars and anchored in ports all round the British Isles, soaked up thousands of boys. They were, in all probability, only a jump ahead of the law and the treatment of them once they were on board differed little from that of the reformatory ship. On a map showing where the ships were anchored and their respective designations, the *Mercury* is listed as one of five for 'Destitute/Voluntary boys'.

The first anchorage for *Mercury* was chosen with care. The old village of Binstead is a little to the west of Ryde in the Isle of Wight, between the main road and the Solent. Most visitors to the island fail to notice it; a lane leads into the village and back out again, it has no obvious attractions, and the beaches on that side of the island are uninteresting and almost inaccessible. Charles and Beatie moved into Binstead House – in effect the manor house for the village – standing between the shoreline to the north and the old village church, which, together with a screen of trees, hid it from prying eyes. They anchored *Mercury* just offshore of the house where she would be afloat at all stages of the tide. There was a ready-made causeway – Binstead Hard – reaching out to the ship. Put there by the Normans, it had served to carry Quarr stone out to the boats that shipped it away to construct old Southampton, Winchester Cathedral and even parts of Dover Castle and the Tower of London. Now it would be a humble ingredient in another small chapter in English history.

Their preparations made, the lovers began a seven-year exile, cut off from the outside world, but near enough to be able to obtain provisions for themselves and their new community.

Since neither Beatie nor Charles had ever been to school they could bring to the running of the *Mercury* a style all their own. It was to be unlike any other school in the country – the traditional boarding schools, the reformatories, land-based or afloat, or any of the residential schools then prevailing, let alone the board schools, with their rows of desks and pupils learning their tables and capes and bays by rote. The staff of instructors knew what skills to impart to their pupils, what would give them an advantage when they joined the training establishments of the Royal Navy or the crew of a rich man's yacht. They might have had strong views on how this should be done, but if they thought they were going to re-create on the *Mercury* the rigours of life on, say, a warship, they were much mistaken, even though the ship had been converted to look like one. Discipline in these early years was going to come not from the threat of punishment, but from example – and Beatie herself was to provide the example.

Out of sheer boredom at being left alone in Binstead while Charles pursued his vendetta with the Gloucestershire aristocracy, she took to going on board the ship every day. Soon she was taking part in the activities there. She set about mastering all the skills of a sailor, bringing to them the same zeal and energy that she had addressed to the business of riding. She took to wearing male attire so that she could go aloft, up the ratlines and along the foot-ropes of the highest yards, nearly a hundred feet above the deck, and she did it in bare feet, winter and summer, with the boys. There were no safety nets. To fall was to risk death or serious injury. The practice continued at least for the boys after the ship was moved to another anchorage with one recorded fatality. The ship's log contains an entry concerning White A.H., Boy 638. It reads 'This boy fell from the main topgallant Jacobs ladder May 17 1898, died instantaneously' *(sic)*.[4]

All this time Beatie trimmed her hair to reduce her femininity, so that people would see her less as a woman striving in a man's world, and more as a person who could succeed across any range of activities open to the young, fit and intelligent. She ignored changing fashions, for to have changed with them would have been to depart from the course she had set herself, consistent in everything she did once she had set her mind to a task, whether it took days or decades to complete. She could row a boat as well as any man – she was still rowing in her seventies – and ferried herself out to the ship every morning to be on deck before the boys got up at six. Their first exercise of the morning – as described by an old *Mercury* boy who died many years ago – was to go aloft, regardless of the weather, 'over the port rigging, at the top by the futtock shrouds, avoiding lubber's hole, and down by the starboard side'. No instructor needed to flourish a cane or a rope's end to drive them on; they responded to Beatie's leadership. The boys swam in the Solent every day, beginning at Easter regardless of when it fell in the calendar and continuing right through to October, and she swam with them. She learned to sail a boat, and forty years later she was still taking boys out on the Hamble in whalers, teaching them the niceties of tacking, gybing and running before the wind. In retirement, one who was on board in the 1920s would repeat her instructions: 'Just before you tack, bear away and pick up a hat full of wind to drive you through.' And then came her shouted order, 'Ready about! Lee Ho!'[5]

As the cycle of training was repeated again and again over the years, Beatie grew more competent than her own staff. She lacked their practical experience of long voyages, being limited to the occasional short cruise on *Diana*, but on the *Mercury* itself, at its anchorage off Binstead, she was supreme. She soon knew enough to hire and fire men without consulting others, and did so until her death, sixty-one years after she had first set foot on the ship.

Very few people outside the ship knew of Beatie's part in its management; none saw her in action. She had become, and would remain all her life, an exceedingly shy person. When a reporter from the Isle of Wight *Observer*[6] was allowed on board in April 1890, Charles showed him round. He found the ship alive with activity. Small boys, newcomers to the ranks, were exercising with dumb-bells in one corner of the main deck, while in another parallel bars had been set up on mats and an instructor was taking older boys through elaborate gymnastics. Lessons in seamanship took place on deck, the whole ship their classroom. Below decks was a classroom in which boys learned to read and write and to handle simple numbers, working on slates. Around the ship there was a constant traffic of boats, some plying between Binstead and Ryde, fetching stores and water, others with boys rowing and sailing as if in constant preparation for a regatta.

Charles continued to leave their island exile to pursue his private war with the landowners of Gloucestershire. He attacked them in letters to the county papers written from Boodles, deriding the efforts of Lord Bathurst to stay in the hunting field with the old VWH. The land he had rented, supposedly for the shooting, now came to the fore in his plan to frustrate the people opposed to him. When boundaries were at last drawn between the territories of the old and the new VWH, some of the landowners found themselves trapped inside the latter and unable to ride across country without permission from the man with whom they were in conflict.

For longer and longer spells Beatie was left in charge of the ship. In the absence of Charles her competence grew: the young woman, still only in her twenties, was setting a style for herself, and for those around her, which would take them through almost to the middle of the next century. When, at the time of her death, boys complained to Mr Fraser about the hardships of life on the *Mercury*, he gave one of the few clues to the extraordinary origin of the regime she ordained when he said that there was no hardship in it that she had not endured herself. None believed it at the time, but research eventually confirmed his words.

Two events brought Charles down to earth and back to the ship for good. Having won, as he thought, a victory over the landowners on the matter of territorial boundaries, he decided to examine the treasurer's records for the previous five years, and calculated that he was owed £3,250 in unpaid hunt subscriptions. When the money was not forthcoming he prepared to pursue the matter in the courts.

Battle lines were drawn, and Earls Bathurst and Suffolk agreed to engage Sir Henry James, who had been Arthur Sumner's counsel in the Court of Chancery, to act for them. (Lord Suffolk, writing to his fellow Earl, said, 'I suspect he would prefer to act for a couple of dukes, but perhaps he will settle for a brace of earls.')[7] With their solicitors they prepared their defence; inevitably there was reference to the scandal and to the case that had been heard in court in March 1885. Charles was furious. To him it was a trick on the part of the earls to deny him payment of subscriptions. All the details of what had happened between him and Beatie would be paraded again, just as he was beginning to hope that the past was over and done with and a new life starting for his second family. His passionate desire to close the doors on the past probably guided his choice of a motto for the ship: 'Now is the acceptable time'. (Beatie, when she took control, changed it to read: 'Men are the souls of ships'.) His solicitors appealed on his behalf for the relevant paragraph to be withdrawn, or, as they saw it, 'to have the action fought on fair grounds'.[8]

By now it was the spring of 1888. Two years of independence with his own pack in what was in effect his own country had brought Charles neither real pleasure nor any perceptible gain. In June Lord Bathurst wrote to Lord Suffolk to say, 'I wish carefully to guard myself from any imputation of over-confidence that the inscrutable Mr. Hoare will drop his action against us, but I think it is probable that his solicitor's appeal was a parting shot on the off-chance of our giving way.'[9] Lord Suffolk, equally cautious, replied that 'I cordially and entirely agree with you. Never Holloa till you are some distance out of a Hoare wood.'[10] In the event, Charles not only dropped the case but also left the county. He loaned his hounds to another man and returned to Binstead.[7]

The second event was a blow from another quarter, finally bringing to an end more than a decade of recklessness. The business world was closing ranks. He was asked to relinquish his post as senior partner in Hoare's Bank. The only surprise was that the request had been so long in coming. On the company's books were the accounts of families related to those whom he had most offended. He had dissipated the equivalent of millions in modern money, and to no very good purpose, unless one sought to elevate the affair with Beatie to a more exalted plane. He was not, however, left destitute. As a senior partner in the bank he could dictate his own terms, and these were enviable: half the profits of the bank for life, and the same to be paid into his estate for a further seven years after his death. The figure involved is said to have been in the region of £40,000 a year, a seven-figure sum today.

In the isolation of Binstead the lovers began to change. Paradoxically, it took the form of a softening of the one and a hardening of the other. The arrogant Charles was to soften into the figure whom C.B. Fry would later describe as possessing 'a genius for kindness', whereas Beatie was to harden into the grim, intense woman who left her mark on the minds and bodies – literally as well as figuratively – of thousands of boys who came into her charge.

For a decade some of these boys and a handful of ex-naval men were to be their only constant company. Charles was to enter on a work of love that would survive him and prove a source of enchantment for as long as there were people to admire artistry and craftsmanship. Beatie, whom one suspects had encouraged the excesses which had brought misfortune to so many, was to find an outlet for the tremendous will she had to shape the lives of others. The Training Ship *Mercury* was to prove too small a stage for her incredible powers. She was a Sara Bernhardt playing a village hall, a Boadicea confined to minor skirmishes.

SEVEN

The Good Ship

The most striking innovation in the new school began innocently enough, yet it brought it into the mainstream of normal life and perhaps set educational precedents.

The boys were on hand twenty-four hours a day, week in, week out, and they needed more pastimes than were at first envisaged. In the evenings especially it was hard to find things to do and they would often sing together, much as the huntsmen did in Cirencester when the rain went on too long. The standard of entertainment went up sharply when James McGavin joined the staff of instructors. Still in his twenties, he came to the ship from his post as director of music at the Theatre Royal, Edinburgh. By the end of the 1880s he had established a military band and a group of string players he referred to as the string band. Every boy on joining the *Mercury* was given the chance to learn an instrument, and they soon proved competent enough to play on bandstands all over the Isle of Wight. At Binstead itself, in the grounds of his house, Charles built a recreation hall so that this new dimension to their lives would have the setting it deserved.

Those who could not master an instrument were encouraged to sing in a choir, and the few who could neither play nor sing were taught to dance, so that eventually the whole ship's company, over 130 boys, was caught up in music-making. Bugles were introduced into the routine and the day began with 'Reveille' and ended with 'Last Post' – the tune of haunting simplicity, valediction to the day, carrying across the water to the house where Charles, Beatie and their little daughter Sybil gathered round an open window to hear it.

Prayers were said in the morning and in the evening on the ship, and hymns were introduced. In the evening the boys sang to the house so that its inhabitants would feel that they were taking part in their worship.

The most notable effect of the new musical life was on Beatie. The tours of Europe with her mother and Uncle Fitz had been unremarkable, travels of the kind that people undertook for perhaps no better reason than to keep up with their peers, to have something to talk about at social gatherings. Now new realms of pleasure were opened to her as McGavin coaxed better and better music from the boys. She would have liked to visit London to hear great orchestras play, but she could not face the risk of encountering people who remembered all too well the events of March 1885, and all that had gone before. But if she could not go to London she would go to the Continent, to Bayreuth. McGavin had opened her ears to Mozart and Beethoven, but above all to Wagner. The huge portentous drama of *The Ring* cycle complemented something in the inner life of the passionate young woman. In time, one of Wagner's operas was to transform her life and that of her lover.

So much was happening on the ship that Charles began the *Training Ship Mercury Magazine* in 1889, with the opening edition covering that and the previous four years.[1] It was printed to a high standard and was for sale outside the ship, the editor advertising that 'subscribers of one shilling and sixpence a year will be entitled to a copy being forwarded to them Post Free every month'. It could hardly be described as compulsive reading, consisting for the most part of a rag-bag of ship's activities, schoolboy jokes and stirring adventure stories in which gallant British sailors weathered terrible storms and defended the British Empire. Sometimes it contained verses written by the boys. One such began:

> I am a Dover lad!
> A happy card am I
> I stand upon the beach
> I watch the sea birds fly.

> I hear great fame about a ship
> That ship I want to see,
> So now I'm off to the Isle of Wight
> To join the *Mercury*.

There were details of entertainments held in the recreation hall, such as 'A short extravaganza written and arranged by C.L. Mackay, in which he will recite the Dagger and Ghost scene from *Macbeth*, followed by "McLean's Musical, Whimsical, and Eccentrical Absurdities"; including a Parody on the celebrated Song "Who's that a-calling so sweet".'

No matter how awful the contents of the earlier editions of the magazine, the delight that Charles took in his latest venture, the care, education and training of boys from the humblest imaginable beginnings, was apparent throughout. The former Master of Fox Hounds was now content to play third man in a cricket match between his boys and 'a team of gentlemen representing the Isle of Wight College'. The man who had stunned Gloucestershire society with his extravagance and insensitivity now watched over his boys with something that resembled tenderness and affection. The instructors he employed drove them extremely hard, but there was no brutality. In a contemporary account of one of the 'entertainments' Charles is described as entering the recreation hall to be greeted from right and left by the boys in the audience, who were all totally unafraid of him, without awe, enjoying his companionship. They owed him everything – the clothes they wore, the food on their tables, the hammocks they slept in at night – but such was his relationship with them that they felt no sense of condescension on his part, and were grateful without having to grovel.

Beatie's part in the life of the ship was never directly referred to in the magazine. But on leaving boys would address their letters of gratitude to her as often as to Charles, and these were printed. In March 1890 a boy who had gone on to the Royal Navy wrote from HMS *Impregnable* in Devonport:

I now take the pleasure of writing these few lines hoping to find you quite well, and to thank you for the kindness of writing to us boys.

I am pleased to hear the ship is getting on so well. I am a Petty Officer boy, and I get on well with my instructions, and I thank Mr. Hoare for the instructions received while I was on the *Mercury*, and I wish I had learnt more than I did. I shall be a first class boy in two weeks' time.

I should very much like a likeness of the racing crews when we had it taken in France, and one of the Ship, if you would be so kind as to send me one; for it brings back remembrance of old times when we were there.

Dear Madam, you must forgive me for not writing before. We all send our respects to you and Mr. Hoare and we shall always be glad to hear the Ship highly spoken of. I must conclude.

I remain, Yours obediently,

S. Cobbledick.

The reference to France in young Cobbledick's letter arose out of the only long voyage made by the ship in her role as a training ship. When Charles finally had to leave Gloucestershire in 1888 he determined to prove that the *Mercury* was no mere showpiece. In October he prepared her for sea, but said nothing to the boys until the day came to hoist anchor. Neither Charles nor Beatie went on the voyage for reasons that remain obscure. The only accounts of what followed are those of the boys themselves, telling in simple language what happened between the first attempt to get out of harbour and their return in April of the following year. Willis, No. 171, describes the first day, 19 October:

The same day as we got under way, we were at dinner, when the Chief Officer, (Mr.) Henderson, came and ordered silence which was immediately obeyed and he said that we was to get under way this afternoon, as soon as Mr. Hoare came aboard to say good-bye to us. At the joyful news, we all gave three cheers, which made the ship ring from stem to stern. The chief officer said we would all be sick before night which I am sorry to say we were.

There was a lot of letter writing to do, to be ready to give to Mr. Hoare, when he came aboard to post for us, and then we began to be restless waiting. About three o'clock Mr. Hoare and Mr. Marshall, the secretary, came on board with some marbles for us to play with at Gibraltar. Mr. Hoare spoke very kindly to us, and pardoned every boy for his conduct, so as he should have as much chance as any other boy. We had six marbles and a glassy each, and with a parting cheer from the rigging, which we had manned, the noble TS *Mercury* hove out of sight, round the point off Cowes, and in a very short time we were flying past the Needles.

A senior boy, John Blackwell, 'Captain of the 1st Division', says that the band was on the poop, and struck the tune 'Good-bye Sweetheart'. He adds that there were 132 boys on the ship and 20 seamen.

Once the voyage had started, there was little or no discussion with the boys on their whereabouts. After eleven days under sail Blackwell writes, 'we turned out at the usual time [and] we were astonished to find ourselves sailing round the Isle of Wight'. The ship was taking in water through a faulty valve, and repairs were completed in Portsmouth, with the ship ready to sail on 13 November. They were towed out of harbour and made plain sail, only to find that the rudder was faulty.

It was 1 December before they finally got away, but even this attempt was nearly thwarted when they had to shelter for five days off St Helens, on the east coast of the Isle of Wight, waiting for a storm to abate. Binstead, their first point of departure more than six weeks earlier, was only five miles away.

There was a desperate quality about the venture after that. Life on deck was so dangerous that the boys spent most of the time below in their hammocks. The ship fought its way across the Bay of Biscay and at one stage was off course, 700 miles deep into the Atlantic. In the port records of Gibraltar[2] the arrival of the 'R.T.Y.C. [Royal Thames Yacht Club] yacht *Mercury*, Capt. W Henderson' is logged for 20 December 1888, a fine sunny day with a temperature of 60° F and the wind W by N force 6.

Allowed ashore just before Christmas Day itself, the boys were befriended by soldiers of the King's Royal Rifles, probably dismayed at the sight of 130 English children drifting aimlessly and unsupervised through the streets of the town. The soldiers invited them to Christmas dinner. They went to the barracks on the day, but stood outside, not sure of their welcome until the soldiers came and 'dragged' them in, as one boy reported it.

We sat down at any table and begun our dinners . . . a lot of officers came into the room and wished them all a merry Christmas. Afterwards we stood up and wished them the same. Beef, pork and potatoes, cabbages, turnips and pickles, mince pies, etc. We eat this with earnest. We had not tasted fresh meat since 30th of October.

They sang and danced for their hosts.

The reference to fresh meat, and the date when last tasted, cast a strange light on the whole venture. It would seem that the boys were forced to stay on board once Charles had committed himself to the idea of the voyage. The delays, which included their return after the eleven days of the first attempt to get away, had brought no relief, though they were in reach of shops and markets crammed with fresh food. Equally strange was the total absence of extra provision on the ship for Christmas Day and the apparent indifference of the men in charge so that the boys had to depend on the kindness of the soldiers. All they had to play with at that festive time was the present of 'marbles and glassy each'.

They set sail on 26 December and on New Year's Day they were in sight of Villefranche, the small harbour to the east of Nice and inside Cap Ferat. There was no shelter from the storm that blew for six days. A tug was needed in the calm that followed to take them into harbour where they anchored among elements of the French, Russian and United States Navies. Officers of the USS *Lancaster*[3] took them under their wing and organised a regatta involving themselves, the *Mercury* and the French ship *Condor*. There was a boat race which the Americans won, but, as a young *Mercury* boy put it 'we was not far behind'. The log of the *Lancaster* states, 'boys from the school ship *Mercury* attended divine services'. It must have been an odd spectacle, the hard men of the naval vessel sharing their main deck with *Mercury*'s crew, some of them tiny figures only eleven years old. Regattas and services aside, the daily routine was as at Binstead, with 'shore leave' on Saturdays.

They left Villefranche mid-March. The voyage home was marginally less hazardous than the outward. Sixteen boys were deemed efficient enough by this time to stay on deck with the men and work the ship in stormy weather. Their arrival at the Rock for water and stores is logged as before, but with no mention of Captain Henderson. There is, however, a 'Mr. W. Hewetson Lt. R.N.' *(sic)* on board.[4] The change in command is just the faintest clue that Charles and Beatie went to Villefranche overland and sacked Henderson.

On 29 March they left the Mediterranean and were making good passage until the wind turned to a gale off Vigo on the north-west coast of Spain. An attempt to make it into harbour failed and they had to ride it out. Waves crashed on the deck and destroyed a cutter that had to be heaved over the side. It was 9 April.

The wind eased the next day and four days of fair winds brought them in sight of England. The timing after that becomes curious: three days sailing to the Needles, the point where they had entered the English Channel on 19 October, and five days before dropping anchor off Binstead on Easter Sunday. There is no talk of being delayed by storms and one can only guess at what happened. In its early days the *Mercury* had two terms, from mid-January to the end of July and from September to mid-December. Men who were on board in those days recalled that Beatie's religious fervour peaked at

Easter and the five days could have been spent lingering in the Channel so that the ship would arrive, symbolically, on the day of the Resurrection, for in the eyes of some it may have seemed that they had indeed come back from the dead.

John Blackwell, 'Captain of the 1st Division', ended the story of the voyage:

We were glad to see dear old England again.

This was the first Training Ship that has been abroad safe and come back again. This was written to show that so young as we were what we had to go through before we were any of us sixteen, and also to say that it is the first Training Ship that ever went abroad. Others have been abroad and never returned, they have either all been wrecked or have had lives lost or some serious damage done to the ship.

And he signed off with his initials: J.B.

In the absence of concrete evidence, one can only speculate about why Charles and Beatie insisted on the voyage going ahead in the dead of winter. Sail training, on ships that actually undertook long voyages, was every bit as hazardous as Blackwell's report. In 1880 HMS *Atlanta* left Bermuda with a crew of 280, most of them boys in their teens, on a training cruise. She was never seen again. In March 1878,[5] HMS *Eurydice* was returning from a similar voyage when she capsized and sank in a squall off the Isle of Wight; only 2 of a crew of 350 were saved. Many bodies drifted ashore or were recovered from the wreck. Among the dead was a distant cousin of Beatie, Lieutenant the Hon. Edward Robert Gifford whose family is memorialised in the church at Berkeley. Beatie may well have attended his funeral, and so knew only too well the risk involved in putting *Mercury* to sea. Charles, with his present of marbles and a pardon for every boy, knew it too. If they were hoping to impress people with the viability of their venture in the wake of humiliation in Gloucestershire and in the banking world, they were doing so at appalling risk to the lives of others. Why did they not sail on the

Margaret Hoare, wife of Charles Hoare. *(Mr and Mrs Tremlett)*

The young Beatie. *(Mrs Hooker)*

Charles Hoare, Master of Fox Hounds for the Beaufort Hunt. *(Mr and Mrs Tremlett)*

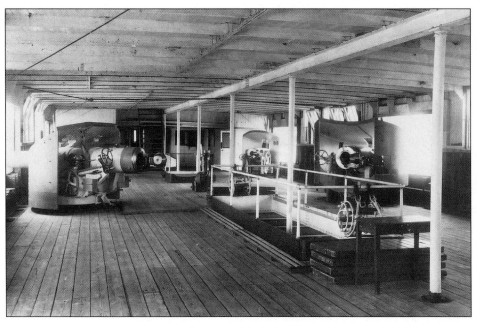

The gun deck, HMS *President*, former HMS *Gannet*, dormitory ship of the TS *Mercury*, from 1916 to 1968. *(Mercury Old Boys' Association (MOBA))*

HMS *Gannet* – later *President* – at the time of her launching, 1878. *(MOBA)*

HMS *President. (MOBA)*

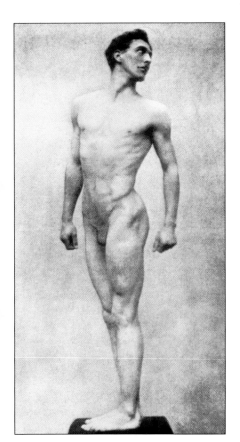

C.B. Fry: the handsomest man in England, '. . . a Greek god, so beautiful in face and body that he might have been wrought by the chisel of Praxiteles, with broad shoulders and narrow hips'. *(Left: Author's Collection, right: J.A. Adams)*

Mercury House, designed by Charles Hoare for his mistress Beatie. *(MOBA)*

The 300-seat theatre, Beatie's Building, 'Dedicated to minds that can soar . . .'. *(MOBA)*

Charles Hoare, the 'old commander'. *(Mr and Mrs Tremlett)*

C.B. Fry – the new commander – *c.* 1912, in the grounds of the *Mercury*. *(J.A. Adams)*

Mrs Fry with her friend, Admiral of the Fleet Sir James Somerville. Left to right: her son Stephen, aide-de-camp to Sir James, Beatie, Sir James, and James McGavin, bandmaster and chief officer of the TS *Mercury*. *(J.A. Adams)*

Winston Churchill, First Sea Lord, came to lunch at ten minutes' notice and inspected the boys in 1914. *(J.A. Adams)*

Mrs Fry hosts the visit of HRH the Duke of York in 1929 in the absence of her husband, who was ill at the time. *(MOBA)*

Beatie *c.* 1912: 'She had calm eyes that looked steadily at people . . .'. *(From* Life Worth Living*)*

The restored HMS *Gannet*. *(Clare Jones)*

ship themselves? Had the whole idea of the school begun to weigh too heavily on people whose lives had hitherto been taken up in a colourful social round? Was their relationship wearing thin, with the need for a release from responsibilities to solve personal problems? The only certainty was that they would never again order the ship to sea.

In the comparative isolation of Binstead Charles and Beatie passed themselves off as a normal family and were known as Mr and Mrs Hoare, but in a census in 1891 Beatie was unavoidably listed under her maiden name of Sumner and recorded as 'Housekeeper'. She was called 'Madame' in her own home, at least from the middle of the Binstead period. This became so ingrained that in time even her own family used this form of address; and C.B. Fry, when he married her, used the word as a name rather than as a title, introducing her to people with 'This is my Madame', and calling her 'Madame' even in their private life. If it served to distance Beatie from the people outside her household, it cannot have lent itself to an easy and affectionate relationship within.

Charles moved his entire establishment to Hamble in the spring of 1892. Seven years of isolation had cooled the passions roused by the 'Gloucestershire Scandal', and they could contemplate an end to their self-imposed exile. Hamble was a more practical site for a number of reasons. Charles still had a business life to pursue, with properties in London and the provinces to control that he could get to with greater ease if he lived on the mainland. And if privacy was important, Hamble, then an obscure little village well away from the main road, provided it. The *Mercury* suffered the same problems as those that beset the officer cadet ship HMS *Britannia*, forerunner of the Royal Naval College, Dartmouth. *Britannia* had been anchored at Portland in 1862, but in severe weather the cadets could be marooned on the ship for days at a time. Within eighteen months she was moved to Dartmouth, which offered not only shelter but also room for the development of a shore establishment. The anchorage at Hamble provided the same benefits for the *Mercury*, which had been exposed to the full force of easterly gales at Binstead.

The move to the river enabled Charles to lay out playing fields, and to put up permanent buildings, classrooms and a recreation hall – important factors, considering the limited life span of a sailing ship.

At Hamble the ship was anchored mid-river, her bows directed upstream. Work began on a twenty-five-room mansion that Charles had designed himself. It was the sort of house he had been accustomed to all his life, with rooms set aside for particular activities, a billiard room, a smoke room, a library and so on. It was a strange pot-pourri of architectural styles, no doubt culled from the many houses he had owned or rented over nearly thirty years. To the trained architect it was not a success; its main features showed little sense of balance or symmetry, and some of the windows were badly proportioned. Charles may not have been all that pleased with it himself, as he sent a photograph to Lady Hoare at Stourhead House in Wiltshire on the back of which he wrote, 'The Institution'.

The main block of The House was four storeys high with a two-storey wing, the lower floor of which contained store rooms, a workroom where boys' clothes were ironed and repaired, and a laundry, while the upper housed a rapidly growing collection of naval artefacts and was in effect a private museum, becoming in time one of the best of its kind in the world. There were models of ships, yachts, paddle-steamers and boats of every description, together with models of typical naval paraphernalia, such as 'Captain Beadon's torpedo-shaped buoy', 'Mr. Hookey's invention for bending planks', and 'Commander Westbrook's standard Tide gauge'.

In the right angle made by the main block and the two-storey wing a conservatory was built which came to be called the 'Veranda', and was used as a classroom. Rustic poles and trellises supporting roses and climbing plants surrounded the space outside, which in later years would become the parade ground where inspections took place. The most remarkable aspect of the whole building was the blend of dwelling and workplace. The stately homes of England – and anywhere else for that matter – are notable for the skill in which design keeps servants and workpeople generally out of sight of the owners. At Mercury House the boys were also the workers and they crowded up to its doors with a select few allowed inside to sweep, clean, bring food from a kitchen nearby and pass it through a hatch in a wall of the dining-room. They paraded in the shadow of the new house and the clamour of bugle calls and shouted orders pervaded its rooms.

The principal room was up an impressive flight of stairs from the entrance hall. It took up a quarter of the floor area of that level of the dwelling and was sited on a corner looking south and west, with a magnificent view of the River Hamble, the Solent into which it flowed, and the constant traffic of ships in and out of Southampton. On the horizon the Isle of Wight could be seen and the New Forest where it came down to the Solent's western edge.

The view also took in almost the whole of the shore site of the *Mercury*. Until the trees and bushes planted in the 1890s matured it was difficult to move about the place without being seen from this room. When Charles died and Beatie took over, there was little doubt that the lace curtains of the windows hid the figure of her in constant vigil when she was not actually prowling the grounds.

Now that she was living on the mainland and closer to the traffic of people, Beatie was more cautious about displaying her athleticism. She was much less active on the sailing ship; her exploits in the rigging and her swims with the boys came to an end, but she still sailed on the river and rowed herself out to the ship. Her manly garb was confined to a floppy bow tie on what looked very much like a man's shirt, but she retained the short hairstyle she had adopted on arriving at Binstead.

By 1896 there was a thriving community ashore and afloat. Lloyd's Yacht Register for that year shows that 'Captain Hoare' had four yachts: *Mercury*; *Pantomime* (153 tons); *Thalia* (13 tons); and *Whisper* (17 tons). All were in constant use: *Mercury* was at permanent anchor and was where the boys slept, dined and did most of their training, while the others served as tenders, taking them on short cruises into the Solent and beyond.

In 1897 Charles and Beatie went to Bayreuth to attend a performance of Wagner's *Parsifal*. Beatie was deeply moved. She protested that it was the music which affected her, but it requires no great leap of the imagination to assume that it was the story as much as its musical setting which stirred her. She could easily identify with Kundry, the 'wild witch upon horseback' of the opera, who inhabited a world of knights and castles, much as the young Beatie had lived among the aristocrats of Gloucestershire in their castles and country houses. Like Kundry, she was an achiever and, like Kundry, she had a dark side.

Charles, for his part, had more than a touch of Parsifal. Ignorant of the world, shut off from reality, first as a boy in Luscombe Castle, and then behind the barricade of money that came soon after, he could be seen as the 'innocent fool' of the story who would attain to a purposeful life only through pain and suffering.

Like Kundry and Parsifal, Beatie and Charles found solace in religion. They contemplated in a new light the enormity of their conduct, of lives damaged by their affair, the relatives in exile and others humiliated by the prurient interest of people in those who had been involved in what was, by Victorian standards, a monumental scandal. Margaret Hoare's every appearance in the hunting field was the signal for crowds to gather for the vicarious thrill of staring at her, a prime victim in the story.

If the lovers could not undo the damage they had done, they could at least begin a new relationship. This they did by living in separate houses, with Charles moving into Hall Place, West Meon, twenty miles from Hamble, an elegant house dating from the early eighteenth century. Then they tried to make the *Mercury* a religious establishment rather than a mere training ship. In Beatie's hands it was not a happy endeavour. Happiness in any normal sense of the word was not her objective. Redemption through suffering was to become the keynote of her religion. The material comforts of her life were considerable, but she drove herself as hard as she drove the people around her. Life, as she was later to tell parents of would-be recruits, was a struggle from birth to Home, a struggle she willingly accepted. She grew in time to merit Lord Roseberry's arresting description of Cromwell as 'a practical mystic, the most formidable and terrible of combinations'.[6]

The first practical result of the visit to Bayreuth was the Building, the name given to the theatre that Beatie had built in the grounds overlooking the Hamble. It was unique in several ways, not least because it was probably the only theatre constructed in the nineteenth century at the behest of a woman and paid for by her, she having sold some of her jewellery for the purpose. Designed by Romanes Walker, it was modelled internally on Wagner's theatre at Bayreuth, the key feature of which is the orchestra under the stage and out of view of the audience. It seated 300 people, though the seating was rather Spartan, and the stage measured 42 feet by 26 feet, fully equipped to deal with the most difficult requirements that an ingenious producer might call for. On an outside wall of the theatre a tablet was installed bearing a dedication composed by Beatie. Carved in capitals, it read:

DEDICATED TO MINDS THAT CAN SOAR, THAT WILL RISE AND NOT BE DISCOURAGED BY OBSTACLES OR DIFFICULTIES, THAT WILL CHANCE AND DARE FOR WHAT THEY LOVE AND KNOW TO BE RIGHT. TO CO-OPERATION, COMBINATION, DASH, PERSEVERANCE, AND UNSELFISHNESS, THIS 'T.S. MERCURY' AND ITS ADJUNCTS ARE FEARLESSLY DEDICATED. FOR HARMONY THE GOOD OF MANKIND AND TO HEARTS THAT CAN BEAT FOR OTHERS. ITS IDEAL IS GOOD FRIDAY'S HERO.[7]

For a while the theatre served as the ship's chapel and a crucifix bearing a life-size figure of Christ was put on an outside wall. In a strange re-enactment of the execution of two thousand years ago, Charles struggled alongside his workmen to hoist the cross and its tragic image into place, the tears pouring down his cheeks. Thereafter, everyone passing the crucifix was obliged to salute it. Inside the theatre there was a reproduction of the Gladiator, the statue found in the Villa Ludovizi that later passed into a papal collection. Its message complemented that of the figure outside as Beatie might have interpreted it, of heroism and of suffering nobly born. It stood on a pedestal at the back of the main auditorium. On it were lines from Byron's *Childe Harolde's Pilgrimage*:

> I see before me the Gladiator lie:
> He leans upon his hand – his manly brow
> Consents to death, but conquers agony . . .[8]

This quotation from Byron, and many others from similarly lofty sources in the footnotes of *Mercury Magazine*, moves one to believe that Beatie did not let the limitations in matters educational deter her from finding her own way. She uses material in ways that suggests she had read original texts rather than taking it from books of quotations. To be well read is not necessarily to be well educated, but it is likely that it was this aspect of her personality that lifted her above the ordinary so that she probably had no problem in holding her own in the company of the many writers who came to her house in later years. There is need also to think on her passion for the music of Wagner. To have gone again and again to Bayreuth to hear music so demanding of its listeners is to confirm the belief of many close to Beatie that she was a woman of formidable intelligence as well as of character.

To all outward appearances the community at Hamble was self-contained, little affected by pressures from the outside world. However, the ship's magazine for 1898 advertised places in the school for those 'able to pay the small premium of £20 per annum, which sum is £10 less than the actual cost of maintaining each boy', a sign that the days of the *Mercury* as a charitable school funded entirely by Charles were over.

Other events were taking place beyond the community that would impinge upon it. Margaret Hoare was living at Kelsey Manor with her mother-in-law, Lady Sophia. All round her the fields were being snapped up by property developers as rural Beckenham turned into

London suburbia, and she decided to leave. She went to Canada to visit her son Wilfred who was working on a ranch, taking Agatha with her; but when they arrived Wilfred told her that they must return at once to England and he would go with them. He was shocked by his mother's appearance, convinced that she was a sick woman. On their return it was found that she had cancer. Charles could not have been indifferent to her suffering, as a reconciliation of sorts took place when Wilfred, who had made his own way in life in the absence of parental help and guidance, was invited to help manage the *Mercury*. True reconciliation took place in 1899 when Charles, urged on by his son, at last made peace with the woman from whom he had so long been estranged. She died on 7 October the same year, and was buried in the family mausoleum in Beckenham.

In June the previous year Beatrice Holme Sumner had married the sportsman and journalist Charles Burgess Fry – 'the great C.B.'

EIGHT

Superman and Superwoman

Ten years her junior, C.B. was twenty-six when he married Beatie. He was the most famous and, in the opinion of many, the handsomest man in England. When the newsboys cried 'Fry wins again!' or 'C.B. scores another century!' people knew at once whose victories were being celebrated.

C.B. was born in April 1872, the eldest son of Mr and Mrs Lewis Fry, formerly of Rotherfield in Sussex. Some of his earliest memories must have been of life in a house near the Chislehurst tunnel in Kent, not far from Charles Hoare's house, Kelsey Manor. Mr Fry was a civil engineer who could afford to send his son to preparatory school, but was probably relieved when, in 1885, the boy won a scholarship to Repton, the public school south of Derby. There he was to manifest that outstanding skill in cricket that was to make him famous. As to his scholarship, it was said of C.B. at Repton that he devised his own curriculum since he was so far in advance of his peers.

After six years at Repton C.B. went up to Wadham College, Oxford. The college had a poor reputation in those days, but in 1891 it attracted a new generation of men so brilliant that their time at Wadham came to be regarded as one of intellectual renaissance. Foremost of these, in addition to C.B., were F.E. Smith, created Lord Birkenhead in 1919, and John Simon, both of whom held the office of Lord Chancellor. All three continued to meet after their Oxford days, Birkenhead and Simon visiting the *Mercury* and becoming vice-presidents – in effect members of the board of governors. Of the three men, C.B. made the greatest initial impression in public life. He had come to the fore as a sportsman at sixteen while still a pupil at Repton, playing for the London Casuals in the FA Cup, the biggest event in the football year. For the next four years he appeared with them, and with the Corinthians and Southampton Football Club, in matches against most of the professional clubs.

During his time at Oxford C.B. rose to be president of the athletics team and captain of the cricket and football teams – honours that seemed bound to accrue to a man who had won blues in all these sports while still only a freshman. A blue in rugby only eluded him when an injury kept him from the critical game with Cambridge. Some observed reluctance on his part to engage in the licensed mayhem of Rugby football where broken noses and misshapen ears were commonplace. The 'Greek god of Wadham', as he was often described, took care of his looks. His tremendous physique was captured in a photograph taken of him to illustrate a book on human anatomy for artists written by Arthur Thomson, Professor of Human Anatomy at the university.

Of all C.B.'s sporting triumphs as an undergraduate the one which brought him greatest fame was the long jump at Iffley Park in March 1893, when he equalled the world record set up by the American C.S. Reber at Detroit in 1891. He was said to have started his jump several inches short of the sandpit rather than risk being disqualified by overstepping the mark. Various stories are told to illustrate his nonchalance in such matters. One tells of his smoking a cigar in the groundsman's hut when the event got under way. He put it down, pulled off his sweater, ran out to equal the record, and then went back to his still smouldering cigar.

After leaving Oxford, C.B. lived precariously in London for a year, which was interrupted by a tour of South Africa to play cricket with a party got together by Lord Hawke. At Oxford he had begun his career as a sports writer with articles in the London papers, but they did not pay enough to give him independence. In another era a man so conspicuously gifted would have attracted a wealthy patron who would have made it possible for him to realise his genius, and the background to his early experiences suggest that patronage in this noblest of senses was his. Without the backing of Lord Hawke, for example, he could never have gone to South Africa.

If there was a downside to his experiences first at Repton and then at Oxford it was the expectations of others. A roll of honour in the Repton School chapel describes him as 'sportsman and scholar'. Somehow he had to make a living in a world in which by education, inclination and popular demand he was the personification of the English gentleman – cultured, urbane, civilised, the acme of good manners – but, like Beatie's father, restricted when it came to ways of making money. In the annual match at Lord's between Gentlemen and Players he wanted, above all, to come down the front steps of the pavilion with the Gentlemen – the amateurs – and not out of the side door with the Players – the paid professionals – since it was his ambition to captain England at cricket, an honour reserved only for the amateurs.

His first job was as a schoolmaster at Charterhouse, a school with a long history of producing leaders and men of letters. He did not take his duties very seriously, and spent a great deal of time in a large barn standing before a set of wickets and getting boys to hurl balls at him as hard as they possibly could so that he could practise endlessly the skills he displayed with such nonchalance and seemingly unrehearsed ease on the cricket fields of England.[1] Aptly enough, he left Charterhouse in the Cricket Quarter of 1898 and went straight to the *Mercury* and marriage with Beatie.

Charles Hoare's passion for cricket undoubtedly brought C.B. into the same orbit. It seems fairly certain that they met when Charles invited C.B. to play at the *Mercury*. Beatie's uncle, Nigel Kingscote, was on the committee of the MCC, so Charles would not be welcome at Lord's, the Mecca of English cricket, but the leading figures in sport could come to him. And an invitation to the *Mercury* would have been difficult to refuse, coming as it did from a man of immense wealth who could entertain his guests lavishly and, for all the scandal attached to his name, was known to be 'well connected'.

Well into the twentieth century it was believed among people who knew C.B. and Beatie that they met in 1895, and that immediately on coming down from Oxford he became secretary to the ship, an appointment that was regarded as a form of patronage, enabling him to take time off to pursue his career in sport in exchange for nominal duties; and that three years of friendship with Beatie, meeting her almost daily when he was not away playing games, mellowed into romance and then marriage. As already observed, there was no secretaryship, and C.B. spent two years at Charterhouse. Another embellishment to the story tells of their having run away from Charles to get married; Charles then sent them a telegram – 'All is forgiven. Come back' – after which, so the story goes, they lived together as a happy trio. This again is unlikely – at least the notion of all three living together – as Charles had moved from Hamble to Hall Place, while C.B. and Beatie, when they did indeed get married, moved into Glenbourne, a house in the village of West End, a few miles from Hamble and Southampton. Cricket nets were set up on the lawn so that C.B. could practise batting. C.M. Sillence, a local historian, gathered stories about the scene. Beatie would bowl to her husband. Her two dogs were trained as 'fielders' to recover any balls that escaped the nets. What shocked her neighbours, however, was her unlady-like manner, bowling over-arm with the skill of a professional. Worse still, her hair was cut short like a man's and she wore trousers.

Nothing seemed less likely than the union between the handsomest man in England and the sturdy woman in Hamble – thirty-six, greying, with her cropped hair and mannish clothes. By the standards of her class Beatie was marrying 'beneath' her. She was an aristocrat; C.B. came from a middle-class family that would not expect one of its members, least of all a man, to marry someone who was related, directly or by marriage, to the likes of the Duke of Beaufort, the Marquess of Cholmondeley, and Lord Bathurst. On their marriage certificate, under the heading of 'rank or profession of father', C.B. entered 'civil engineer', while Beatie wrote simply 'gentleman'.

If they differed markedly in appearance and origins, they were also distanced by their differing intellects. C.B. was a brilliant

Oxford graduate, with an acute mind that absorbed without effort whatever subject took his fancy. When, in December 1908, he became Captain Superintendent of the *Mercury* in succession to Charles Hoare, his academic subjects listed in the staff records were 'Greek, Latin, Moral Philosophy, Ancient History, French, German, Spanish, Mathematics, Physics and Naval History'.[2] Beatie, like most of her peer group, had never been to school, never mind university, and there is nothing to suggest that she was tutored at home. As her husband's interests were expanding, hers were contracting, making the ship the centre of all her energies. They might have found common ground in a shared interest in outdoor pursuits, but for Beatie the outdoors was the ship and the waters of the Solent and the Channel, demanding a love of the outdoors for its own sake, whereas for C.B. an open stretch of sky was incomplete without an audience to watch and applaud. Beatie was becoming reclusive. C.B. was a showman almost all his life.

As to why they got married, only they could have answered such a question, but there appears to be no record of their meeting, courtship, marriage or the nature of their relationship thereafter. A cynical version was that Charles Hoare persuaded C.B. to marry the lady in order to protect her from the icy blasts of society after his, Charles's, death. C.B. in return would have a sinecure for life, the captaincy of the *Mercury*, which his wife would run for him. It could be argued that she, who had flouted society for so long, married at last for the sake of respectability. However, there may have been much less of a gulf between the newlyweds than appeared on the surface. If C.B. was the Superman of late Victorian England, Beatie was the Superwoman, the fearless rider to hounds whose skill on horseback as much as her striking looks and charisma had attracted one of the richest men in England. At the *Mercury* C.B. would have seen her prowess in another element, as she rowed and sailed on the river with practised skill. She might even have surprised him by swinging aloft 'over the port rigging, at the top by the futtock shrouds, avoiding lubbers hole'. By comparison the other women he could have married might have seemed effete.

Their characters, if different, were complementary. C.B. was a man of action, but only in the public arena in which he enjoyed so much success. Away from the public gaze he was elegant, witty, brilliant – but not practical. Beatie, one suspects, would not have wanted a practical person to share the niche she had created for herself, someone with whom she might have to argue about the practicalities of running the ship. The fact that his wife was older than he might well have appealed to C.B. Together they wrote a pallid novel called *A Mother's Son*, and the title may hint at the sheltering role that the older Beatie played for her young husband, protecting him at times from the demands of a public that craved greater and still greater achievements from its idols.

The marriage took place on 4 June 1898. A girl was born in February 1899 and christened Charis. It was an unusual choice of name. In Homer's *Iliad* Achilles loses his armour when Patroclus wears it in fatal combat with Hector. Thetis, mother of Achilles, hastens to the home of the gods to order new armour from Hephaestus, 'Smith to the gods', goldsmith and also a worker in fine jewels. She finds him busy riveting handles to twenty three-legged cauldrons, attended by his wife Charis. He moves about on a chair fitted with golden wheels which, at a nod, takes him to wherever he needs to be, for Hephaestus is a cripple, and Charles Hoare, descended from horse dealers and the goldsmith who founded Hoare's Bank, was partly crippled, with legs that were not the same length. C.B., the Oxford classicist, would not have missed this sly intimation of the baby's parentage, one that suggests a subtlety of thinking not usually attributed to Beatie. In appearance Charis had the heavy features and build of Charles Hoare, and not the leaner, aquiline of a Fry. There were to be two more pregnancies – Stephen, then Faith, who was born in 1910 when Beatie was forty-eight. All five children went to the house at West End.

For the next ten years Charles controlled the *Mercury*, commuting from West Meon to Hamble, while C.B. stayed in the wings as far as the ship was concerned, and Beatie played a less dominant role there, awaiting the time when she would take over. It was a time that Stephen, born in 1900, recalled with pain and bitterness when he spoke about it a few months before his death in 1979. Before going to boarding school, and then in school holidays, he was left at Glenbourne with servants and to the untender ministrations of his teenage half-sister, while his father pursued a busy life in the public eye, and his mother continued her obsession with, as Stephen described it, 'her ship'.

Life in the public eye included the zenith of C.B.'s cricketing career in partnership with the Indian prince Kumar Shri Ranjitsinhji, Jam Sahib of Nawanagar – 'Ranji', as the public called him. They vied with each other in setting new batting records: in 1901 C.B. scored 3,147 runs in first-class cricket, including six centuries in successive innings. He also continued to play football at national level and was the only man alive who could play in a Cup Final on a Saturday and on the following Monday take part in a first-class game of cricket. His cricketing career was – and still is – the subject of debate among enthusiasts with controversy about his seeming inconsistency in performance. The possibility of his private life as an ingredient in this has to be considered.

Meanwhile, Beatie continued to appear at the *Mercury*, though her role for the time being was secondary to that of Wilfred Hoare. She is seldom mentioned in letters and other accounts of life on the ship at this time. In the summer she went to cricket matches with her husband. Whether it was at Lord's, the Oval or a county ground far from home she would sit with the public most of the time and join him after the game to deliver pungent comments on his performance.

Charles Hoare was now in the last decade of his life, freed from his former mistress but not unconcerned about her. Within the ship things went on as before, with Wilfred Hoare sharing the administration with his father. The religious life, which had become so important, found a place of its own when Charles designed and built a chapel.

The new chapel was built of wood clad in metal, with the sheets of metal hammered onto the overlapping planks to retain the impression of a timber construction. (It was dedicated to St Agatha, reputedly a Sicilian woman of aristocratic descent; she had been pursued by Quintian, a man of consular rank, who caused her death by torture when she refused his advances.) An Anglican priest was employed as a permanent chaplain to the ship, and the full ritual of the church was celebrated daily.

The atmosphere inside the chapel was one of intense gloom, with the choir screen and internal fittings and walls varnished or painted in dark colours. The windows were of clear glass, but these had been made opaque with coloured images in imitation of stained glass.

The unceasing stream of activity for the boys continued – sailing in the various tenders of the parent ship, drill in all the nautical skills, and games of football, rugby and cricket at home and away with teams from as far afield as Taunton. They went on forays into the surrounding countryside on bicycles that Charles provided. Occasionally they went by launch to Portsmouth and Gosport to visit the naval training establishment to which most of them were headed. And all the time there was the background of music, in the chapel and the theatre, and from bugle calls that punctuated the day, summoning them to meals, bidding them to be still and hear an important order, and to carry on after it was delivered.

Among the visitors to the ship in the opening years of the new century was Harold Begbie, a journalist with the *Chronicle*, a London newspaper. He used to bring with him his daughter Joan, who was born the year Beatie and C.B. married. Far into adulthood she continued to visit and was briefly employed to teach art. In 1980 she remembered these visits with clarity, beginning at the time when Boy Mogg was assigned to amuse her. He took her for rides on the model train that Charles had built in the grounds for amusement and to carry stores to the pier for transport by boat to his yachts. Mogg pushed the little girl along in an open truck, as he was not allowed to operate the steam engine on his own. Boy L.G. Charles, No. 904, also remembered the Begbies, and how Harold in one of his articles in the magazine *Sunday At Home* described the *Mercury* boys as 'the happiest in England'. In 1974, L.G. Charles, then eighty-two years old and living in retirement in Canada, described life as a *Mercury* boy in 1903.[3] The place was an odd mixture of tough ship and progressive school. The boys still rose at six and went up the rigging in bare feet, but no longer with Beatie to lead them. They came ashore for showers and a breakfast of cocoa and ship's biscuits before attending lessons in classrooms close to The House. There was physical training in a gymnasium and band practice in the theatre. At noon everybody returned to the ship for a midday meal, and in the afternoon there was rowing, sailing and games. Evenings were full of music, and a long day ended with Last Post at nine. When L.G. Charles went on to describe the punishments, the reader might have expected harsh beatings, matching the hardy lifestyle of the boys.

Instead the accent was on rewarding good behaviour, with boys able to earn up to a shilling a week if they could avoid 'demerit marks' to spend in the tuck shop on 'packets of candies, or allsorts as they were called, jam, jellies, or condensed milk'. The hectic pace of the day was such that deprivation of sleep was the ultimate and most effective punishment. A bucket of water was placed on the starboard side of the poop deck, an empty bucket on the port. After the others were in their hammocks for the night the miscreant had to transfer the contents from one to the other using an egg-cup. The night officer put a chalk mark inside the rim of the full bucket, so it was impossible to get away with pouring it into the empty one.

Whereas the younger boys were given the bucket-and-egg-cup punishment, the older ones were 'sent truck from nine to midnight'. L.G. Charles got two sessions of this, one for wagging his ears in chapel and making the other boys laugh, the other when he was working in the galley and slipped on the gangway as he was on his way down to empty some slops into the river. Captain McKenzie, a senior officer, was on his way up at the time, and the boy knocked him overboard. Boy Charles threw him a rope, which was promptly used to give the galley-boy a beating when the dripping officer got on board, a rare instance of corporal punishment, though the offender considered it deserved. The truck is the highest part of the mast, a hundred feet above the deck on a ship the size of the *Mercury*. Boy Charles went up the rigging in the dark, but sneaked up with him a canvas sling he had improvised so that he could tie himself to the top few feet of the mast and doze in safety till the order came for him to return to the deck.

When, in 1974, the old seafarer reflected on his years at the *Mercury* he did so with unmistakable pleasure, unaware of the grim place it was to become after the founder's death. He remembered the names of his former shipmates, most of whom he hadn't seen for nearly seventy years, 'Hollis, Bonner, Trevor, Mogg', who had been happy with him under Charles Hoare – 'the Old Commander' as he called him.

The Old Commander was still playing cricket for the ship when he was sixty. The year was 1907. In nearby Southampton the Hampshire County Cricket Club had made him their chairman, an honour that capped a lifetime of devotion to the game. He bought a Rolls-Royce, and in it he went further afield to watch his club play or to collect more ship models for his little museum. Energetic and outgoing, his horizons had expanded in directions unimaginable ten years earlier. At Hall Place, his house in West Meon, he met members of his family and entertained intimate friends, but his former mistress and her husband did not appear there. Harold Begbie stayed there with his wife and children. To Begbie's daughter, Joan, it was a second home where she even had a small cart drawn by a Shetland pony for her own use. In 1956 a journalist writing in a Southampton paper spoke of 'the white-haired imperious Charles Hoare';[4] yet in 1980 Joan Begbie spoke of a gentle man, with a deep calm voice, who never raised that voice or his hand to a child.

To Hall Place Harold Begbie brought Arthur Mee, the brilliant Nottingham man who's *Children's Encyclopaedia* and *Children's Newspaper* won him so much acclaim. Together the three men, Begbie, Mee and Charles, talked about education and how much more could be done for children, and Charles heard the journalists advocate ideas which came close to the system he had evolved on the ship where pupils achieved without those in charge having recourse to the repressive measures that were common in the schools of the day.

In the closing weeks of 1907 Charles, rich, admired and now deservedly respected for his work at the *Mercury*, was seen at the ship for the last time. He attended the Prize Day ceremonies on 21 December. Two days later he went to Hindhead, ill and in search of a change of air to improve his condition. From thence he went to Brighton, but returned at last to Hall Place in February. In April he took to his bed, stricken with cancer. His son Wilfred, christened 'Father Wilfred' by the Begbie children because of his gentle, priestly manner and appearance, deputised for him at the ship. The leather-bound collection of *Mercury Magazines* for 1908[5] record the minutiae of ship life for that year, interspersed with comments of growing concern about 'our beloved Commander'. Only rarely do the Frys appear in its pages, such as when C.B. gave each boy a present of a book entitled *What Nelson Said* – 'a nice kind present', according to the editor of the magazine.

A peculiarity of the magazine is that each page bears a footnote, sometimes literary in origin, but often of the 'improving' kind. 'Push forward!'; 'Persevere and never fear'; 'Speak of a man as you find him'; 'Quietness is best'. Reading these footnotes with the knowledge that the editor knew Charles was dying, one is inclined to believe that his failing health was traced in them, even while the main text tried to strike a hopeful note. Thus in January Charles is reported as 'happily now recovering', while the footnote reads 'One is not as soon healed as hurt'. In March he is reported as ill, but we are reminded that 'Love can vanquish death'.

A busy life went on in his absence. In February the chaplain, Mr Blofield, and the chief officer, Mr Bartlett, were out all day with a group of boys, shooting and ferreting. They bagged eight rabbits and a weasel. During some bright days in early March the cricket pitch was rolled and boys tended their own gardens. Their pets –

rabbits, mice and bantams – were doing well, but 'one of Moulton's goldfish died'.

St Patrick's Day was Wilfred Hoare's birthday and there was a concert of Irish music in the Building to celebrate the day and honour the Commander's son. They gave him three hearty cheers and a chorus of 'For he's a jolly good fellow!' March ended gloomily when Boy Garner Wakefield, No. 966, died in Southampton Hospital after a short illness. His body was placed in the chapel and boys were appointed, two at a time, to watch over him until his funeral the next day. After the service on Saturday afternoon the coffin was placed on a gun-carriage drawn by his shipmates. They made their way to the cemetery preceded by a firing party and the band playing 'The Dead March' from *Saul*, so completing a full military funeral, even to the volleys fired over the open grave.

April was cold, and there was a confusion of blossom and unseasonable snow. In the magazine the editor, on behalf of the boys, spoke to Charles, who was sure to get a copy: 'They want you back, sir, they miss you . . . they love you.'

There were rehearsals that month for a performance of three scenes from Verdi's *Il Trovatore*. Easter Sunday fell on the 10th, and they sang the 'Hallelujah Chorus' from Handel's *Messiah* in chapel after the evening service.

May began with cricket matches; there was much excitement on the 16th when two yachts, the *Barbara* and *Allegro*, went aground in the River Hamble and the boys helped to refloat them.

Charles's birthday fell on 18 May. Beatie, aware how close he was to death and unable to visit him in Hall Place, made a gesture which would tell him of her love and sense of grief. She gave him a present of a sick communion set. This was delivered to her at Hamble and immediately taken to the chapel and placed in the Tabernacle on the high altar. The set, as its name implies, was used to take communion to the sick or to give the last rites of the Church to someone who was dying, the priest obtaining from the Tabernacle the consecrated ingredients of the ritual and the vessels of the set in one small container – a box for the bread, a bottle filled with wine, a chalice and a paten, all made of silver. It was used that same week to give the last rites to Charles.

He lay in a bedroom with four windows through which he could see a copper beech, with all its portents of spring's early promise, summer's fulfilment, autumn's mellow harvest, and stark winter that ends the cycle – and yet begins another. At the foot of his bed was a little kneeling desk. Beyond this, on the wall, was a crucifix with palms on either side, remnants of that year's Easter celebrations. Here the set was used, bearing him not just the last rites of the Church, but also the love of the woman who had transformed his life.

Charles died at 9.30 on the morning of 22 May, four days after his birthday, a pale, thin, wasted shell of the powerful man he had once been. The May edition of the ship's magazine carried a description of him as he had been before illness overcame him. Beatie had composed the dedicatory lines that appeared on the wall of the Building that includes the words 'To hearts that can beat for others'. The echo of this phrase in the verbal portrait of Charles suggests that she was its author:

> Height 6 ft 1 in, of noble width in proportion, two good feet carried him, he himself used to say one of his legs was shorter than the other, consequently he walked a little bit late. His hands were always flat and thin rather delicate long-fingered sensitive hands. His chest was abundant and gave his splendid heart room to beat for all. Here was a personality who walked straight on, with a round head crowned with pure white hair. When well his was a rosy face, an absolute gentle firm mouth with two deep lines on either side, a pair of shrewd observant blue eyes set very deep and overhung with the bushiest golden eyebrows. Two well-set ears, which heard every sound, and a beautiful dear kind fore head furrowed with deep lines and a frown.

Tears were shed for him on the ship and at his funeral. He was buried in West Meon churchyard. Eighteen boys acted as pallbearers. The thousandth boy to enter the ship followed the coffin. This was a significant gesture. Even before he met Beatie, Charles had shocked his father and the other partners in Hoare's Bank with his extravagance. His father was said to have urged him to make amends by educating a thousand poor boys at his own expense. The boy following the coffin signalled that the debt had been paid.

C.B. was at the funeral, but not Beatie, though she may have visited the churchyard secretly before the ceremony, the *Mercury Magazine* carrying a description in her idiosyncratic style of the open grave with the pile of excavated chalk, brilliant white on the dark green grass. A simple Celtic cross was later put on the spot on a rise of ground south and a little east of the church. It bears the name of the dead man and the dates of his birth and death. Nothing else. If epitaph was wanting it could have been a footnote from the magazine: 'Life is a long lesson in humility'.

Thus died one of the most extravagant characters of the time, a peculiar mixture of paradoxes, half bluster and half Victorian refinement, a man who spent the early part of his life ruining the lives of others, obliquely or otherwise, but who mellowed into middle-aged kindliness. Thirty of these years were spent with Beatie. Their life together seems to us to be curiously public, until one remembers that our principal mementoes are newspapers, law reports and the fading memories of the very old, and the private was deeply hid, as is true of most lives. If we are left to guess at what drove them, there is at least one tribute to the intensity of their relationship – the episode in Cecily Hill House when they wept before Arthur Sumner and his efforts to prise them apart.

Publicly Charles had run the gauntlet of society's disdain, to be followed by years of devotion to the ship, the two periods united by his passion for the girl he had met on the hunting fields of Gloucestershire. His love for her was so circumspect that he may indeed have colluded in her union with C.B. Fry, bringing the two together so that Beatie, the 'fallen woman', would be sheltered from the scorn of society after his death. It was a union that, in denying him her company for much of that time, gave him time and space in which to make some kind of peace with himself and with the world. In the end, though much of the damage he had done was irreversible, he won through to such a surprising degree of respect from all sides that his obituarists could honestly describe him as a humble and compassionate man. One of them, attempting to find words to describe a man who was so generous with his life, as well as with his money, wrote that 'It was the poor who loved him so. Them he understood so completely. Here was a socialist, who carried socialism right up to the front with majesty.'[6] The young coachman, the 'gallant Master of Fox-hounds', as he was so often called in hunting reports, the banker who had tried to burn money faster than the firm could make it, had come a long way.

His will was long and labyrinthine. He left an estate of the gross value of £234,256, many millions in today's money. All his children were provided for. Sybil and Robin, his children by Beatie, were as well provided for as those born to his wife, Margaret. To his daughter, Agatha, he left Hall Place, the house in which he died. He exercised his right to appoint one of his sons to a partnership in the bank in Fleet Street, but none of them took it up. Ralph, Robin and Reginald were abroad, and Wilfred, who had helped him run the ship, had shown little interest in the family business. It was revealed that as far back as 1886, the year the VWH split, Charles had set up trust funds for Beatie and Sybil, the incomes from which they would receive after his death. No figures were given, but in 1936 Beatie was able to make her own will, leaving investments and property that reflected his generosity. While Beatie's monetary legacy from the will was a mere – but discreet – £300, the entire contents of The House were hers for life, to be passed on after her death to Robin and Sybil. In the unlikely event of the *Mercury* being closed or sold to other people, Beatie was to have the value of the theatre – £1,360, the amount it had cost to build.

Despite his concern for the security of his former mistress there is an interesting codicil to the will. He had bought a house in Salcombe in Devon for 'Mary Beatrice Perch (widow)' for £1,800, a sum out of all proportion to the figure one might leave to a loyal servant or housekeeper. James McGavin, for example, got an annuity of £20. Had Charles found someone to comfort him in his declining years, someone less overpowering than the formidable Beatie?

There was a long clause in the will in which the future of the *Mercury* was discussed. Charles intended that it should have money from his estate to cover the running costs for two years, during which time his trustees should try to find 'some public body or institution or some person or persons to take over the said training ship', together with his collection of ship models and marine artefacts. It had been hoped that a firm legacy in favour of the ship and the people running it would assure the future of the whole enterprise. At first glance this reservation is puzzling. When these details of the will were published there was a brief flurry of legal wrangling from which C.B. emerged as a suitable 'public person', able at least to run the ship for the two years covered by its late founder. Within six months, aided by a newly formed governing body, C.B. had collected £2,000 in subscriptions and donations, enough to persuade the High Court to establish the *Mercury* as an educational charity under his direction. Whatever his reservations about leaving money to run the ship, and even supposing his feelings had cooled towards Beatie, Charles had said in his will that 'I particularly recommend that my trustees do employ the said Beatrice Holme Fry . . . as manager . . . of the said training ship either for such remuneration as my trustees may think proper or without remuneration.' Her husband's role in this was to appear as Captain Superintendent and enable a woman to command an all-male establishment at a time when most women were confined to roles that were menial, domestic or decorative. His reward was a lifelong sinecure and the freedom to enjoy his life as cricketer, journalist and public figure. He now had all the trappings of a 'gentleman' – a twenty-five-room mansion luxuriously furnished, spacious grounds, a Rolls-Royce and even, to begin with, a butler and servants. He could entertain in style his wide circle of acquaintances – F.E. Smith, John Simon, the Churchills, Kipling, Baden-Powell, Lord Halifax and many more. In time he would pay a bitter price for all this luxury, but to begin with all he had to do was let Beatie run everything as Charles had intended.

NINE

The Gun

Changes were bound to take place when C.B. and his wife moved from Glenbourne to Mercury House, the official residence of the Captain Superintendent of the TS *Mercury*, but for a year at least the brisk but friendly atmosphere which had been the hallmark of Charles Hoare survived.

In *The Captain*, one of two magazines published at the time and edited by C.B., an article appeared about the ship written by A.B. Cooper, who visited the *Mercury* in May 1909. It describes a household as opulent as some of the great country houses of the time. The boys seem a jolly lot, moving at a lively pace through an exciting routine in their novel surroundings with the beautiful barque-rigged sailing vessel on the river, and the spacious shore establishment dominated by the magnificent theatre – the whole, ashore and afloat – referred to simply as the *Mercury*. Like other guests he might have been taken to see them shower. As they left to dry themselves they would pass before the duty officer and each one would raise his arms above his head and pirouette for top-to-toe inspection, a practice that persisted for the rest of the Fry era. There is a suitably flattering portrait of C.B. extolling his charm, erudition and commanding good looks, and a short aside on the character of his wife: 'Mrs. Fry . . . is the soul of things. She has the loving heart, wise brain, and the kindly eyes, which see and understand, which feel and know, which plan and sympathise.'[1] This may have been an oblique way of informing the reader that Beatie was the guiding force behind the running of the place, but the time was swiftly coming when none of the warm adjectives would apply, at least not in the minds of the young people who were about to feel the full blast of her direct rule. She may, for all they knew, have been loving, wise and kindly, but if so these traits were well concealed.

A photograph of her taken about this time conveys much of the character found by Lytton Strachey in the face of another formidable woman, Florence Nightingale. There is the same 'serenity of high deliberation in the scope of the capacious brow'. The eyes reflect the 'sign of power', 'the traces of a harsh and dangerous temper' that Strachey read into the face of his subject. 'There was humour in the face, but the curious watcher might wonder whether it was humour of a very pleasant kind; might ask himself . . . what sort of sardonic merriment this same lady might not give vent to, in the privacy of her chamber.'[2]

For a year at least C.B. exercised some authority, and thereafter took part in the day-to-day running of the place when it did not interfere with his public life as sportsman, journalist, and bon viveur, much in demand in the homes of the great and the famous. In January 1909, a month after he formally took up office as Captain Superintendent, a future Commander RN, A.E. Horrell, joined the ship. In his eighties Horrell retained clear and affectionate memories of a man who could take a class on most subjects and inspire his pupils by his command of them. Sadly these occasions were few and irregular, but the possibility that the permanent member of staff might look up from his work to find C.B. hovering in the doorway, ready and willing to take over the class in an instant, served to keep the standards high. When he was at the *Mercury* in 1914, Reggie Sinfield, Boy No. 1391, saw the great man teaching seamanship and signals, but C.B.'s enthusiasm for teaching of any kind, other than on the playing field, seems to have been short-lived. Certainly it had evaporated by the end of the First World War. Inevitably the sporting life of the ship received most of his attention – it was openly admitted that a new instructor or even a carpenter taken on the staff might get the job in preference to other applicants if he could play cricket. In the summer boys queued up at the nets to bowl to one of the greatest batsmen ever to take to the field.

For a select few there was a chance to play in his team at a weekend match that might include some of the finest players in the world, such as 'Plum' Warner, Philip Head and Ranjitsinhji. It is not surprising that some boys developed a lifelong passion for the game. Bill Mobsby, Boy No. 1846, managed to return to the *Mercury* in later years to play cricket, and Reggie Sinfield went on to become a professional and to achieve fame as the man who bowled out Bradman in the 1938 Nottingham Test.

As her husband's enthusiasm for the steady routine of running the ship declined, Beatie took firmer control – as Charles Hoare had always assumed she would.

The appointment of C.B. as a commander in the Royal Naval Reserve brought about a shift in emphases at the *Mercury*. From then on the ship flew the blue ensign of the RNR and not the red ensign of the Merchant Navy, complemented in early days with the flag of the yacht club of which Charles was a member. It also brought the school in line for Admiralty inspection. In other similar pre-sea schools this could mean an inspection by someone appointed by the Admiralty. Beatie's aristocratic connections meant that an admiral would inspect, and preparations for such occasions were intensified beyond anything that had previously applied. There were rewards. Most *Mercury* boys arriving at the main training establishments of the Royal Navy were graded as Advanced Class. This meant that they had arrived with skills in seamanship, rifle drill, signals, and swimming, together with competency in the basic subjects of education, skills they would otherwise have to acquire before training as a specialist in one of the many departments of a warship. The agency that had made this possible – in this case the *Mercury* – received a bounty from the Admiralty, a sum of money that varied over the years from £15 to £25 per boy. The Navy had been saved the cost of three months' training. In good years there was an income of over £1,000 a year from this source. There was, however, a downside to the arrangement. No concession was made to those who were preparing to go into the Merchant Navy, and they spent great swathes of time in developing skills for which there would be no practical use when they left the *Mercury*.

Under Charles Hoare life on board had been strongly influenced by his special relationship with the boys in his care. They were like an enormous family that needed a high level of discipline, if only to bring order to lives sometimes spent in crowded conditions in boats or on the ship on the river. But there was also room for individuality, with pets and garden plots to look after and bicycles to ride in the lanes outside. Under Beatie all these were abolished. Her regimentation of life on board quickly became total. She had a loathing, containing in it a distinct element of fear, of boys being idle or even momentarily out of her control. If they were not being eternally marched from one activity to another by her staff, then they had to march each other. A group going from the main building to the bucket lavatories – the 'heads', in nautical parlance – at the foot of the playing field would identify, in the absence of a member of staff, the most senior of their number and then allow him to march them to the heads and back. Occasionally the more spirited of their number would satirise this aspect of ship's life. Two boys, given permission to use the heads, would decide which was the senior and he would tell his companion to 'get fell in', call him to attention and then direct his squad of one to its destination, subjecting it to the full barrage of imprecations learned from the ex-naval petty officers who taught them drill – 'You 'orrible lot! Get in step! Pick yer feet up!'

The element of fear in Beatie's mentality stemmed from the very real danger of the enterprise failing and leaving her at the mercy of a world that still knew too much about her past for comfort. She could quiet these fears by making the ship so successful that her way of life and her livelihood were secure. She could also cut herself off from the world – a device that meant cutting the boys off from it as well. If they wandered into the village or spoke to outsiders they might learn about her past, and thus erode her authority and, worse still, her security. And so began the burden of constraints that would weigh heavily on every generation of boys from 1909 until death relieved Beatie of all her earthly worries.

There were other innovations that served to tighten Beatie's grip on everybody. In- and outgoing letters were read by her and Sybil. New boys were told bluntly that any unfavourable references to the ship would result in their letters being stopped. Boys had been numbered from the time the school was founded, if only to serve as a running record of how many had passed through. Now they were addressed by their numbers at all times, wore them conspicuously on the backs of their shirts, and used numbers instead of names even among themselves, if only because an instructor might send for '578', and the messenger would have to know to whom these digits applied. Friendships were regarded as subversive, but few were formed because there was no time to spare in which to cultivate them. Bullying, so common in most residential schools, was remarkably absent. As one old *Mercury* boy commented, each boy was too busy keeping his own yard-arm clear – i.e., keeping out of trouble with Beatie.

Curiously enough, in spite of her fears, Beatie entered on two practices that emphatically kept alive memories of Charles Hoare. Every Saturday she and Sybil drove in her Rolls-Royce to the churchyard in West Meon. They took gardening tools with them and tended his grave. What Beatie's husband felt about this weekly pilgrimage has not been recorded. This went on for many years and an immediate result of it was that Charles's daughter, Agatha, sold Hall Place and left West Meon for good. To be deprived of her father in his lifetime had been a burden. To have his grave tended by the woman who was the author of this was intolerable.[3]

The second practice was one of keeping unoccupied the seat Charles had used in the chapel – the middle chair in a row of five, six rows from the front on the south side of the aisle. A shallow bowl of flowers was maintained on it for the next forty-two years.

One of the first problems Beatie had to solve on taking over in 1908 was to find a replacement for the sailing ship *Mercury*, now over forty years old and presenting problems familiar to the owner of any yacht. Repairs and maintenance were costly, so much so that the bills threatened to be greater than the actual value of the ship;

and even when they had been completed, its value was still decreasing with age. An application made by Charles Hoare some years earlier to the Admiralty for a replacement was revived and they offered HMS *President*, a drill ship of the RNR. More time went by without anything happening when, in 1914, there was an unexpected visit from the First Lord of the Admiralty, Winston Churchill, accompanied by his brother Jack, Admiral Hood and F.E. Smith, whom C.B. had known at Oxford. Despite a mere ten minutes' notice, the ship's company was mustered and ready for inspection on their arrival. So impressed was Churchill by the boys and the establishment that he was ready to act on the request for the ship. Within a few weeks HMS *President*, formerly HMS *Gannet*, was towed down the Channel by the battleship HMS *Queen* to Portsmouth and then by tug to the Hamble. For two years the two ships dominated the river, the sailing vessel, her elaborate rigging still intact, dwarfed by her neighbour with her high ugly superstructure, though the *President* was in fact only 30 feet longer than the barque.

The sailing ship *Mercury* – the former *Illovo* – was sold in 1916 to a Mr David Petrie for £1,250 and converted into a coal hulk.[4] She was taken from the Hamble river in September to Harland and Wolff's shipyard at Southampton and stripped of her masts and rigging. This was the fate of many ships – coal was still the prime source of energy for most powered ships, only a few warships of advanced design being oil-fired. The hulks – the Royal Navy called them 'coal haulabouts' – provided a means of storing fuel that was cheap and flexible. Instead of paying to go alongside a wharf to load fuel, a ship would tie up alongside a hulk and take the coal from there. Alternatively, a tug would bring the hulk to the ship.

Both Beatie and her husband romanticised her life and death. C.B. wrote of her as she had been when she was carrying cargo as 'searching for wind in the China Seas'. In fact her longest journey had been to the coast of East Africa by way of the Cape of Good Hope. Beatie preferred another's words to express her feelings, quoting in every edition of the Prize Day programme for years the lines written by Gregory Robinson entitled 'The Good Ship'. Robinson was a marine artist of some note who lived in Hamble village. He wrote, 'It is many years since she glided down the straight ways into the grey North Sea, the pride of the man who built her – a ship with a fine entry and a clean run.' There follows a passage in which the writer traces her career, coming at last to rest in the River Hamble. Hundreds of boys are trained in her before she is taken to the shipyards to be converted to a coal hulk. Her death is described in anthropomorphic terms. Feeble and old, 'she dipped to the sea, but could not lift, and the waters closed over her'. He concludes: 'So she passed into the quiet starlit waters of Memory there to wait for orders. And there for us she remains until the stars pale to gold; then those orders will come, and she will lay a course for the Islands of the Blessed, there to join company with all good ships and enter the Splendid Haven.'[5]

These slightly fanciful words were seized on by Beatie, who could not imagine an ignominious end to the ship at the heart of her struggle for personal freedom. For the end, as far as it can be traced, was just that. In 1917 she was under tow, loaded with coal, in or near the port of Cardiff, and foundered in a sudden squall when the tow-rope snapped. At a time when the newspapers were crammed with news of a terrible war, the loss of a mere hulk went unnoticed.

With the departure of the old sailing ship most of the daily routine now took place on shore, with meals being served in a new dining-hall. More buildings would be added over the years. The ship on the river was little more than a floating dormitory, one that had to be reached every night regardless of the weather.

When the First World War ended, forty-six old *Mercury* boys had died in action. Their worth, and the worth of hundreds of others who had served with them, and had been hammered into seamanlike material by Beatie, was recognised by the authorities responsible for awarding service decorations. She was appointed 'Officer of the Civil Division of the Most Excellent Order of the British Empire' – the OBE – in the Birthday Honours List of 1918. As a girl she had never made her debut at Court, as would have been normal for a girl of her background. Now she went to Buckingham Palace to receive her badge at an investiture held on 29 October. King George V, from whom she accepted the decoration, knew about her from his father, Edward VII, and may have visited the *Mercury*, details that would not emerge until nearly the end of the twentieth century. This single event shattered the myth of her joint captaincy with C.B.; the bizarre episodes of her young life were discreetly forgotten, and the doors of the great houses of Gloucestershire opened to her again. Six years later Lord Apsley, the grandson of Lord Bathurst, the man who drove Charles Hoare out of the hunting field, was guest of honour at a Prize Day and joined the distinguished list of ship's vice-presidents.

In 1918 recognition came to Robin Hoare, the second of the two children born to Beatie and Charles. After attending the Loretto School in Edinburgh he drifted. Old *Mercury* boys, recording their memories in later years, remembered him as an enigmatic youth who owned his own yacht. He would appear on the river mysteriously one day, stay for a week, and just as mysteriously disappear. At last he went to New Zealand. He stayed there for a few years before working his passage home via Valparaiso – where he took charge of a string of polo ponies for delivery to an English port – arriving in time to join the Navy at the outbreak of hostilities in 1914. Between April and August of 1918 he was awarded the DSC, the DSO, the Albert Medal and a bar to the DSO. His contemporaries described him as a man completely without fear, seeking dangers and going into them against a stream of men fleeing for their lives.

Beatie seemed to wield authority with an even greater confidence after receiving the OBE. The symbol of her authority – appropriately enough – was the gun. A 6-inch breech-loading weapon, it was cemented into a low platform in a corner of the gymnasium, its barrel pointing through a gun port which could be opened and closed in much the same manner as the gun ports on the *President*. It had been put there for drill purposes, so that teams of boys could gather round to load it with dummy shells, 'fire it', and extract the 'spent' shell cases as they would on the warships they were to join later. In fact it was the centrepiece in the ceremonial beatings that became a feature of ship's life soon after Beatie took over. For ten years the man in charge of punishment was Arthur Ward, known behind his back as 'Sharkey'. He was thirty years old when he joined the staff in 1914.[6] A former petty officer, he had served in the main training establishments of the Royal Navy as a physical training instructor, the hardest of the hard men who ruled the lower deck of the service and reputed to have been dismissed from the service as being too tough even for their tough company. He was a short, extremely powerful man, dark-visaged, with a grey, menacing jaw. The subjects he taught were officially listed as 'Seamanship, Swimming, Wrestling (two styles), Fencing and Boxing', but his main function was to be the instrument of Beatie's rule, to thrash (not to put too fine a point on it) the school into submission. In the 1980s, men who had suffered under him were bitter in their recollections. Though able in the evening of their lives to shrug off the hardships and vicissitudes of decades at sea, they harboured nevertheless a detestation of the man as livid as the weals he had once left on their young bodies.

Beating was the punishment for a wide range of offences. Merely being a nuisance was enough to earn a trip to the gun. For boys who were caught stealing there was no escape, but they were so hungry that they still took the risk, looting the vegetable garden in which their more fortunate predecessors had worked their own plots. Running away was considered the worst offence, so that the boy who most feared the regime was the prime victim of its severity.

Beatie decided who was to be beaten, 'awarding' – her word – the number of hits with the cane. When a boy was due for punishment it was announced at breakfast on the day it was due to take place. In 1921 for example, No. 1766, J. Isaacs, was awarded twelve strokes across the gun 'for being a General Nuisance'. After breakfast the ship's company marched to the gymnasium and were formed into lines to witness punishment.

Some of their possessions were stored in the building. Their 'ditty' boxes, small wooden containers holding a few personal items, were on shelves along two of the walls. Their wet-weather clothes – oilskins and sou'westers – were hoisted to the ceiling on clothes racks; one of these was lowered, and a few garments were removed and thrown over the breech mechanism of the gun to protect the genitals of the victim from injury. Meanwhile, Boy No. 1766 was conducted to a changing room where he was made to strip naked and then dress in a pair of thin white cotton trousers. When he entered the gymnasium he walked past his assembled shipmates and mounted the gun platform. He stood facing the gun, the barrel pointing away from his midriff like a huge steel phallus. Behind him and to his right was the duty officer, a clipboard in his hand bearing a paper, a flysheet with full details of what was about to take place. 'Sharkey' stood to his left, holding a thick, almost inflexible cane with decorative twine wrappings at its extremities.

The charge was read out and the number of cuts. The greater the punishment, the more likely it was Beatie would be present, standing by the main entrance, looking across the heads of the boys to see that it was done. 'Sharkey' ordered the boy to bend over the gun, and on the order 'Carry on!' he struck with all his might. The instant the blow fell, 'Sharkey' would decide if his victim could stand the rest without flinching. Often he could not, and the man laid aside his cane and with short cords tied the boy's ankles to rings on the platform, and his wrists to the gun-carriage. 'Sharkey' then took up the cane and continued his work, placing every blow in a different place to maximise the pain. He smirked as he struck, seeming to enjoy his work. He put his full strength into the blows, just as he had when caning grown men in the Royal Navy, even though his victim could be a boy barely into his teens. The duty officer ticked them off on his flysheet, and Beatie watched impassively. The grim evidence was there for all to see in the showers the next morning.

Those who could survive without cries or tears, and without the indignity of being tethered like a wild animal, turned on their tormentor and gave him the look of utter contempt they felt he deserved. When it was over the boys left the gymnasium in cold fear of the man who had done this thing – and of the woman who licensed him to do it.

C.B. took no part in this, though he could not have been unaware of that which took place under what was ostensibly his authority. What he could not have envisaged, when he became Captain Superintendent in order to allow his wife to become manager, was that Sybil and Charis would join her as deputies in the enterprise. In the 1920s, when he was often away for months at a time, the place was run entirely by these women. Sybil policed the establishment, ashore and afloat, on behalf of her mother and was greatly feared. All too often when one was spreadeagled over the gun it was on the strength of her reports. The instructors feared her too, resenting the power she exercised over them, but although they were helpless before her they pitied her the long hours of drudgery she suffered, supervising the laundry where hundreds of garments were washed every week, and undertaking a host of other menial tasks. She, of aristocratic descent, dutifully inspected the lavatories. Charis worked in the office. Gentle and more kindly than Sybil, boys wrote to her after they left, much as they used to write to her mother in the early days, and she answered them like a favourite aunt, concerned about their welfare, applauding success, commiserating failures. Faith was too young to be involved in administration, but as an excellent musician she took part, along with Charis, in the rich musical life of the ship. Her mother provided her with a violin by Joseph Cagliono. She was made to practise for hours every day as if in preparation for a professional career, but nothing came of it if only because it would have meant leaving home to study. In common with their mother, none of the three daughters went to school. None of them would ever marry.

Stephen came home immediately after the First World War after serving in the Royal Navy as an engineer officer. He had trained at Osborne, the short-lived naval college on the Isle of Wight where he was a contemporary of the future Admiral of the Fleet, Lord Mountbatten of Burma, but he disliked the whole business of life at sea, and resented being forced into it by his parents. He made no pretence at being able to order boys about, nor did he have any desire to instruct except on the cricket field or in the theatre, where he too joined in the music-making, but it cannot have given him much pleasure. A *Mercury* boy of that era described him and his sisters as 'drifting about the place like disconsolate wraiths'. His position was unenviable. He had neither his father's brilliance nor his mother's character, and since their interests were elsewhere – his father leading a busy life in the public eye, his mother obsessed with regulating the lives of 'her boys' – he was left to his own devices. For years he lived a shadowy existence with no firm purpose, eventually going into journalism and the Civil Service. Had he written his story it would have been revealing on the subject of what it was like to be the son of formidable parents, and a gentle man in a hard school run entirely by women.

TEN

'Make him Bleed!'

By the mid-1920s three decades of care and attention had mellowed the shore establishment from a bleak slope going down to the Hamble to a small park with trees and well-tended gardens. A rough rectangle of forty-five acres was bounded on two long sides by Satchell Lane and the Hamble. Of the remaining sides, the one nearest the village extended from a letter box on the lane down to the river, while the fourth separated the grounds from open country, which in those days stretched with little interruption to Bursledon, a couple of miles upstream. A tiny stream bisected the site. On one half stood the buildings, on the other, that nearest Hamble village, the sports field. Charles Hoare's 'Institution' had ivy growing up the walls in places and trees close by which helped to soften the outlines. At the point where the sports field began to slope suddenly down to the river stood the tall signal mast. Near this was a pergola of rustic poles covered in climbing roses which Beatie had planted and which she maintained, as she maintained most of the gardens close to her home. Not far away, at the bottom of the same slope, were the heads, the bucket lavatories, like a row of sentry boxes, doorless, the only concession to privacy being a nail at the entry to each on which the occupant could hang the numbered wooden tag which entitled him to the use of the correspondingly numbered lavatory. You walked behind the box with the tag on show. Against the hedge nearest Satchell Lane stood a small cricket pavilion.

In 1980, elderly men who had trained at the *Mercury* vividly recalled their experiences of Beatie in 1920. Ernest Walker represented the new type of boy who entered the ship after the First

113

World War. They were no longer 'improved street arabs' to be saved from 'temporal and eternal ruin'. Many were the sons of resourceful parents who were ambitious for their children, and went about the business of realising those ambitions with determination. Ernest's background was comfortably middle class, with family money coming from ownership of textile mills and Manchester cotton-broking. He could have gone to the costliest boarding school in the land, but chose instead the *Mercury*, as did many others, because of the aura of C.B.

In August 1920 Mr and Mrs Walker and their son arrived by taxi at the gate on Satchell Lane nearest the ship's chapel. They walked along the drive that took them behind The House. Coal had been delivered, and a pile lay on the ground by the basement hatch. They heard the noise of shovelling from below and called for directions to the office. A woman appeared, holding a shovel. She was dressed in a navy blue jacket and skirt. She told them the way, and when they reached the place they were met by Charis, who was then joined by her mother, still grimy from her efforts in the basement. At fifty-eight Beatie was as strong as a horse and ready to turn her hand to anything.

If their first feelings for the lady were of admiration, these were dispelled by the events of the next half-hour or so. In his seventies Ernest remembered the occasion:

She spoke to my father briefly, then called to a passing boy and told him to take me to the gymnasium. This he did, carrying my suitcase. In the gym was an officer; I seem to remember that it was Mr. Reid. He told me to tip everything out of my case, and then he began stencilling my number on my clothes. He produced a kit-bag and tipped out its contents: a complete naval uniform. He told me to change into it. This I did, then he sent for a chair. He told me to sit in it, and taking one of my towels to put round my shoulders, he proceeded to clip off every hair on my head! Yes, I began to weep quietly. I was only fourteen years of age and this was my first time away from home. I felt I was being reduced to the state of a convict.

When this was finished he told the boy to take me back to the office. When my parents saw me my mother burst into tears at the sight of my hairless head. In those far off days hair was kept short. But now I looked as if my head had been shaved. My father demanded of Mrs. Fry the reason for this barbarism to which he was told more or less to mind his own business, that it was essential in the maintenance of cleanliness for all boys to have their hair short. My father observed that my hair was not just short – there was none! But he was not enlightened further, and very soon the time came for my parents to leave. We made our farewells amidst more tears and I could see that my father was furious; he felt he had handed me over to something more akin to a Borstal institution, the place reserved for youthful criminals, than a naval training school. He told me to write and let him know how things were, but I was never able to do this, because Mrs. Fry told me that a letter containing criticism would be destroyed, and I would be severely punished.[1]

The school year was divided into two terms, from mid-January to early July, and from late August to mid-December. In the term beginning January 1921, Walker reached such a low ebb that he asked to speak to C.B. The face at the office window demanded reasons, but he would not give them. At last he was allowed to enter the great man's office and was received with kindness, heard with sympathy, and given gentle words of encouragement and a look of such compassion that he was able to return to the ranks and see out the long dreary term to the end. When he got home his health had been so impaired that the family doctor instructed his parents not to allow him to return. Ernest went on to a career of high adventure, serving in the RAF, prospecting for gold in Canada, exploring in the Arctic, organising his own Antarctic expedition (only to have it frustrated by the start of the Second World War), fighting in Crete, being captured by German paratroopers and then proving so habitual an escapee that his captors often had to put him in chains; but for now he had had enough.

The pace then – as always – was unrelenting, with 'Sharkey' Ward to the fore in the race to keep the boys not just busy, but harassed to the point of exhaustion. He would take a crew of boys rowing in a cutter down to Southampton Water and back, driving them as if they were able-bodied seamen and not mere boys. He strutted up and down the boat, from thwart to thwart, a rope's end in his hand to beat them about the shoulders when he thought they were slacking. On shore he was in charge of boxing lessons in the little cricket pavilion. The lessons were simple and direct, which is to say that he took on the whole class, one at a time, and battered them. Only once did he get his comeuppance. A boy who could take no more got up from the floor, dazed and bloodied, and grabbed a broom that was propped against the wall. He brought the handle down on 'Sharkey's' head, a smashing blow that cut him to the bone and required twelve stitches to close it. The boy went to the gun, but perhaps wisely 'Sharkey' never laid a finger on him again.

His reign went on for several more years. On 6 September 1922, he was administering a 'shake-up' on Beatie's orders, making the boys run round and round the playing field carrying rifles over their heads, or at full arm's stretch in front of them with one hand, and then in the other. When boys began to collapse, 'Sharkey' beat them with the rope's end and forced them to keep going. When Boy No. 1927, Geoffrey Petch, collapsed there was no response to the blows or the orders. He was carried to the veranda, and from thence by ambulance to hospital and died soon after.

In the 1990s elderly relatives told of Geoffrey's having endured – even revelled – in the hardships he encountered in his first year on the ship. There were, however, misgivings at the time about the circumstances of his death. The death certificate, under the heading 'Cause of Death', reads 'Appendicitis 6 days. General peritonitis. No P.M. [Post Mortem]'. He was, it would seem, victim of the practice of punishing boys who reported sick as being suspected of malingering.

There was no ceremony for the dead boy, no night in the chapel with his shipmates to watch over him, no gun-carriage, no bugle calls or volley over his open grave. In the ship's log there are a few laconic words: 'Died whilst under training at the RSH Infirmary, Southampton. He is buried at Hull.'[2]

Dreadful though this episode might seem in modern eyes, it created surprisingly little disturbance at the time. It was not reported in the newspapers, for example. 'Sharkey' had been an instructor at HMS *Ganges*, a land-based training ship. There he had seen boys of fifteen and sixteen die 'whilst under training'. They lie buried in the naval cemetery attached to Shotley parish church, side-by-side with sailors and marines killed in action in ships off the coast of East Anglia. Today it is a place of such tranquillity that one cannot begin to imagine the violence it took to fill so many graves.

Equally tranquil is the grave of Geoffrey Petch who is buried not 'at Hull', but at Hedon a few miles to the east of Hull. He had lost both his parents, mother in 1912 and father in 1916. Uncles, aunts and grandparents combined to bring him up. He was descended from the Heron and Iveson families who had lived in the village for centuries. The men had been craftsmen who built many of Hedon's houses, one of which Geoffrey would have inherited had he lived. A brilliant child whose enthusiasms included cricket and wireless – he was building his own sets at a time when most were still being built by amateurs – he had been offered a scholarship at Hymer's College, Hull, a prestigious grammar school. He could, if he chose, use the scholarship to attend the *Mercury*. Pictures of famous cricketers adorned his room, C.B. among them, and it was no surprise to his family when he chose to be at the place captained by his hero, the great all-rounder. When his body was returned to Hedon for burial it was with the information that he had died of appendicitis. There was no mention of the circumstances.

The most incredible aspect of life on the *Mercury* was that much of the punishment handed out was for unspecified offences. The 'shake-up' that killed Petch was a sharp reminder of who was in charge as much as anything else, but if an explanation were given it was that boys were getting 'slack' and needed something to make them 'taut' again. On the veranda Beatie kept a notice board with a list of defaulters. It was up to each boy to read this every day to discover if he was in trouble. The list merely indicated the offenders and the punishment, never the offence, even supposing there was one. To appear on the list meant a spell of running barefoot round a flinty track in the vicinity of the signal mast where boys waited for their turn at the heads. Up to the early 1920s, the mast itself was occasionally used for a variant of the punishment on the old sailing ship of 'going truck till midnight'. The ship's company would assemble in the morning to see one of their number, dressed in thin cotton clothes, forced to climb to the cross-trees, over 50 feet above the ground, where he stayed for the whole day without food or drink. It was not unknown for a boy in winter to become so cold and frightened by the end of the day that his mates had to climb the rigging to help him down.

Another old *Mercury* boy who recorded his experiences on the ship was Commander Henry Gardner, who had a distinguished career in the Fleet Air Arm from which he retired to a house in Victoria, British Columbia. When he died in 1979 his widow presented the manuscript of his unpublished autobiography to the National Maritime Museum, Greenwich.[3] Like Ernest Walker, he recalled life on the ship in the early 1920s, having gone there partly with the assistance of a Council scholarship. His father earned £150 a year, but so highly did he value the prospect of his son getting the start in a naval career which the *Mercury* seemed to offer that he willingly made the sacrifices needed to kit out his son and to pay the fees outstanding after the scholarship money had been spent.

Young Gardner's first encounter with Beatie was marginally less traumatic than that of Ernest Walker. In the company of his mother he presented himself at the office and 'through the window there peered a large red face framed in short grey hair'. The face addressed him 'in a booming baritone voice' and sent him off to change into uniform and have his hair shorn. Once again there followed the insensitive business of presenting the boy to his mother, who was predictably aghast at the transformation that had taken place.

What Gardner experienced in eighteen months on the ship was so extreme that, like everybody else, he found the Royal Navy by comparison rather lax. He vividly recalled the first hour of the day that was spent on 'clean ship', scrubbing and polishing with the fervour of those who knew that Beatie and Sybil would inspect their work, and that the gun awaited those whose work was unsatisfactory. As a boy he could only guess at how heavily the authority of these women weighed on the men who worked for them. Their children often had to play in the ship's grounds so as to get a glimpse of their fathers in term time, and their wives endured loneliness comparable to that of women whose husbands were at sea, for there was pressure on the staff, especially the senior men, to work inordinately long hours. Since the boys had to be driven relentlessly from six in the morning until nine at night, somebody had to be on hand all the time to see that this was done. It was not enough merely to be on duty. They had to provide visible proof of having pushed the boys to the limit. An instructor called 'Stumpy' Childs had the boys scraping the surface of the deck under their hammocks with their bare hands for any stray bits of blanket wool that had escaped the brooms on the days when the decks were not scrubbed – a process called 'fluffing'. The men invented new punishments, or turned a mundane task into something so exhausting that it constituted a punishment. Billy Reid, a seamanship instructor as well as being handy with the clippers, devised a senseless exercise called 'luffs and tackles'. A ship's tackle, used for lifting heavy weights, was spread out on the ground and, instead of weights, boys were attached to it, pulling against each other in a hopeless tug-of-war, while Reid set about them with a rope's end.

The dining-hall, which might have provided an oasis of relief in the avalanche of activity that constituted the day, became instead a battlefield. On every table lay a utensil that symbolised the daily struggle for survival – a soup ladle, heavily dented. As the longest implement to hand, it was used by the section leader as a club to beat anyone who stepped out of line by not working hard enough to satisfy the impossibly high standards expected of them here as in every other part of the ship. Something as simple as singing grace before meals, usually a verse from an infant hymn, had to be done to perfection, with several repeats if need be, while the food on the table got cold. Once seated, the utensils they ate from were a further source of dismay. In the 1920s porridge was eaten from wooden bowls with wooden spoons. To those who needed every ounce of food going they were an abomination. It was difficult, short of using fingers or licking the bowl, to get every last vestige of food off the wooden surface and into one's mouth. The bulk of each meal – a sort of dietary backbone – consisted of a long loaf of white bread, though for reasons never made clear there might be a loaf and a half or, very rarely, even two loaves to a mess, the name given to the group of twelve boys at each table. One person cut the bread into slices with the ritual precision of one who knew he would get the last pick and, if he miscalculated, the smallest slice.

Once out of the dining-hall and on to the next stage of the day's routine, the hazards multiplied. The standards of dress and appearance were, like everything else, almost impossibly high, in some instances because the means of achieving them were always in short supply. For example, having perfect bootlaces was absolutely essential, but if a lace broke or somebody stole it, it could not be replaced. It was forbidden to go to the village to buy another pair, and no laces were sold on the ship, yet no excuse of any kind was accepted if a boy reached an inspection with these items missing. Punishment followed as night follows day. The misery bred by what was no more than a minor inconvenience was incalculable. The loss of a lace reverberated through the company as the victim hunted for another, and if successful, either by violent appropriation or simple theft, set off a chain reaction in the ranks. It was almost as if Beatie had set them at each other's throats, men and boys alike, as part of a scheme to dominate their lives at all times.

Even the few moments of leisure were beset with hazards. It was forbidden to slump down, to loll, to fall asleep or simply 'cave in' when a rare break in the routine occurred. In summer, when C.B.

included a couple of boys in a cricket team, which otherwise was composed of the top players in the country, the rest were obliged to sit around the edge of the field and watch. They had to sit bolt upright for hours, arms crossed in front of them. They were, as one of their number put it in later years, like rabbits mesmerised before a stoat. Beatie and Sybil kept watch, and the first to waver was the first to get a verbal lashing, with the promise of something nasty to follow from the long list of punishments available. The cricket pitch itself had been brought to perfection by miscreants lugging a heavy roller backwards and forwards over it until they were limp with fatigue.

Surprisingly, there was the occasional moment of relief from all this. Colin Ridge – the boy who had cracked 'Sharkey' over the head with the broom handle – remembered Thursdays, when the tuck shop opened and sixpence would buy a pound of broken biscuits. Afterwards there was letter-writing followed by an evening in the theatre:

> At six o'clock we'd march into the theatre and sit in dead silence with folded arms. Suddenly the lights would be extinguished and there on the screen amidst rapturous applause would appear the caption 'Harry Burrel, a real regular fellow and owner of the Bar H Ranch'. If Stephen Fry's arm ached from hand-cranking the 35mm projector for two hours he had succeeded in making Thursday a happy day.[4]

Time spent in the Building was treasured not only for the film shows, but because it brought the boys into contact with men who differed markedly from the ex-petty officers who formed the bulk of the instructional staff. The bandmasters were also ex-servicemen, usually from Royal Marine bands, but their discipline, in the sense of mastery of a given subject, put them in a totally different category. To begin with, their subject gained them special favour in Beatie's eyes, since music was associated with her spiritual aspirations. Nor could it be presented with the shouts, insults and blows that accompanied a lesson in gunnery or boat drill. If a boy felt he was being bullied he ran no risk if he stopped making progress in the subject; he was merely passed over as tone deaf. He might redeem himself if he was good dancer or could sing. Inevitably a large number of boys responded to treatment that differed drastically from that experienced on the parade ground or on the river. Success led to other pleasant diversions. The tradition of the school band playing on bandstands in the locality continued. Together with the Fry children, boys entered competitions in music festivals, usually in Winchester; they returned with prizes in music and country dancing, and had their successes recorded in local newspapers as well as in the ship's magazine. R.E. Hutchins, who rose to high rank in the Royal Navy, went even further afield, accompanying Stephen Fry to London. Stephen gave a piano recital in the Rudolf Steiner Hall of music by Debussy, while Hutchins provided visual accompaniment, projecting light onto a screen, the beam bouncing off a tray of water that rippled in time to the music. Another boy played trumpet so brilliantly that he was rewarded with a bed in the servants' quarters of The House. In the evening he went on board the ship in the river with the ship's company and returned after he had played 'Last Post', turning a call that had become boring with repetition into a melodious fanfare. Other performers were persuaded to stay beyond the expected date of leaving in order to play in a particularly important concert or to impress a visiting admiral.

For many boys the chapel became a place of sanctuary. There was always an Anglican priest to officiate at the services, and without exception they were kindly men who won respect for their ability to make the chapel a true haven, and for being undaunted by Beatie. One suspects that they tempered the harsh life of the *Mercury*. They had to accept the rule of compulsory church attendance imposed by her, but to a man these priests insisted that attendance at the three-hour-long service on Good Friday be voluntary and there were to be no recriminations against those who did not attend. Year after year, the chapel was packed on that sacred day. Three hours of music, prayer, sermon and Bible readings were preferable to most things that could take place outside. Beatie, of course, was there and took the Sacraments, as she did at every opportunity during the rest of the year, always kneeling at the same place by the altar rail; but for once nobody trembled at her presence.

The sports field provided a diversion for some boys, but not as much as it might have done in a conventional school. It used up precious energy, and playing at anything less than full tilt was regarded as a sort of moral crime.

Famous visitors to the ship brought some relief. It was exciting to meet, face-to-face, such heroic figures as Evans of the Broke, who was in command of HMS *Broke* in 1917 when she rammed a German destroyer at twenty-seven knots. Shackleton, the explorer, came to see them before his last voyage to the Antarctic and spelled out what it took to survive in that terrible place. Dunbar-Naismith, who had taken his submarine through the 'impenetrable' Dardanelles and bombarded Constantinople, sat at the front of the stage in his frock coat with sword on hip and told his story. There was little doubt among those who knew of Beatie's origins that the distinguished visitors were honoured – even excited – at the prospect of fulfilling her invitation to speak at the *Mercury*.

A frequent visitor in the 1920s, staying for weeks at a time with the Fry family, was Clara Butt, the singer, when she was performing at theatres on the south coast, and she often appeared on the stage of the theatre. After one of her visits, she left behind her son Victor – reputedly uncontrollable at his regular boarding school – who was made to join the ranks as he was said to be in need of discipline.

The Building, the chapel, the playing field and the famous visitors – these brought some relief or colour to a world of iron discipline. Without them life might have been intolerable, but even so there is hardly a page in the register for that time, ten names to a page, without two or more entries of boys leaving before completing the course of training. Reasons are given, like 'Unsuitable for training', or 'Withdrawn by parents', but, as in the case of Ernest Walker, they were, more than likely, boys who were broken by the system.

Beatie drove herself as hard as she drove the boys and her staff. She rarely left the premises. She was up before everybody, and in winter she lit the fires herself. She did not rest until 'Last Post' was sounded, and the lights went out on the dormitory ship. She shared some of the hardships inflicted on the boys, sleeping in an unheated room with the window open all the year round. After her death, her room was cleared and a pigeon's nest was found on top of the wardrobe. She did not baulk at physical labour, as Ernest Walker discovered, and was often to be seen engaged in work she could have delegated to a labourer from the village. The war memorial, the little brick clocktower, was commissioned by her, but she dug the foundations herself. She was in her seventies before she gave up rowing boats on the Hamble. E.P. Hunter of Exeter, Gardner's contemporary on the ship, remembers her as being dressed in a long ankle-length red serge skirt, a much-worn cardigan, a leather belt with a bunch of keys swinging from her waist, an old apron, and heavy brogues over darned woollen stockings.[5] She prowled the grounds relentlessly, and not until he was in his hammock did a boy feel safe from her. Commander Gardner said of her that she had a habit of popping up anywhere and everywhere, always with some fault to find. Her outstanding characteristic, he felt, was an ability to discern moral turpitude in even minor faults. The assumption was that 'ordinary decent people always behaved in a way that was utterly honest and honourable. This meant that any boy whose behaviour fell below this artificial norm was rotten.'

Although the boys could tell something about Beatie's character and behaviour outside her house, they knew very little of her life inside it. A favoured few got as far as the pantry, and were responsible for carrying meals up from the galley, putting dishes on hot plates, then keeping out of the way until it was time to wash the dirty dishes and claim as their rightful 'perks' any food left over. Occasionally a member of staff lodged in the servants' quarters – perhaps a night officer who slept during the day – but he had no part in the private life of those whose home it was. He might witness curious events, but he would be unwise to discuss them outside.

Gardner guessed at another world beyond the office, where the Frys lived 'the gracious life of country gentry'. It was a good guess, confirmed by the accounts of people who were the guests of C.B., cricketers and sports writers mainly, who enjoyed lavish dinners that seemed to take hours to consume.

One man who reported an encounter with Beatie in her private domain was A.L.E. Hoskyns-Abrahall, a former naval officer and a future bishop. He met her in the large room overlooking the veranda, the eyrie from which she could observe most of what went on in the grounds. He described a long well-lit room, its walls covered from floor to ceiling with pictures, photos mostly, largely of men, many of them signed. They represented the great and good who came to see for themselves one of the most remarkable women in England, and yet one of the most secretive. She would hold audience, seated in a deep leather chair, with visitors sitting around her in rapt silence. They hung on her every word as she ranged over the personalities of those who had come her way. Whether she was right or wrong in her judgements did not matter. She had spoken, and the judgements would stay for ever in the minds of her listeners. Hoskyns-Abrahall remembered a time when C.B. was present, sitting alone, ignored and disconsolate at the far end of the room from those clustered so intently about his wife.[6]

Visitors came in their greatest numbers in the long summer holidays. Joan Begbie described the time. Empty of boys, the buildings and grounds were a source of wonderment – The House itself, the little museum, the superb theatre, classrooms and dining-hall, the gym with the gun in the corner, the spacious grounds with the cricket pitch rolled and ready for use, and the dormitory ship. On hot days the ship was magical, especially to the young. It had secret places out of bounds to those who slept there during the school year – a long tunnel that once held the propeller shaft, dark compartments below the waterline where stores and ammunition were kept in its time as a fighting ship, a ladder that went from the tunnel to the open space where the great bronze propeller was housed when she was under sail. There were little cabins where the handful of officers used to live at one end of the ship, and gloomy cramped quarters at the other for the hundred or so sailors. *Mercury* boys had got into the sailors' quarters at some time in the past, lighting their way with candles. These they had used to burn their numbers on the insides of lockers. The vast spaces of the orlop and upper deck, dormitories in term-time, were ideal for ball games if the weather turned nasty. When the tide was right people swam in the river, diving off the stage on the port side. The Fry children led the way for the dare-devils, up the ladder to the roof and along the long walk-way to a point where they could get to the figure-head on the bow and dive off it into the water between the anchor chains. The supreme test was to jump off the roof itself, a height of over 30 feet. There were small boats and the cutters for rowing and sailing, and never a thought that these resources, the things from which they derived so much fun, were the trappings of the hard lives of their regular inhabitants.

The holidays over, Beatie returned to work. She placed notebooks in all the places where boys cleaned, swept, scrubbed and polished, in which they reported on what they had done and – if they were in charge of a team – commented on the work of individuals. She read these every evening, adding her own terse comments on what she had seen during the day. The list of boys who had been to the lavatory was carefully examined. Only bowel movements were recorded. If certain names – or rather numbers – did not appear routinely in this notebook, those concerned were not being 'regular' and were likely to get a dose of suitable 'opening' medicine. Visits to the heads were timed, and those who took more than five minutes had TLH – 'Too long at heads' – put against their numbers. This made her suspect the boys concerned were perched over their buckets for some more recondite pleasure, and their numbers went straight into the defaulters' list.

Whereas in most schools pupils take home reports intended for themselves and their parents to read, Beatie would publish her comments on boys in the ship's magazine that she edited. The magazine was for sale to parents who must have wondered at the extraordinary things she said about their sons. Sometimes she

126

introduced the boys by their numbers, sometimes by name. In a 1928 edition she added their nicknames – 'the Owl', 'Hurricane Ned', 'Stonehenge' and 'the Gimlet'. Her remarks ranged from the whimsical to the waspish:

2127 Needs rhythm in his life and to love, keeping in touch with the sun and the moon and all big beautiful creations and going joyfully with these.[7]
2163 He must keep very young and learn to sing well songs that would charm fairies into listening.[8]
2187 A patient boy who needs masses of warm sunny air to close round him and make him feel how beautiful a wealth of beauty strewn indiscriminately for him can be, and to be content. He swims.[9]
2305 Indescribably idle.[10]
2417 He lacks any vestige of humility, a want which is so confusing as to make one mentally deficient[11]
2463 He holds himself and his powers in very high esteem. As a talker he is a maniac.[12]
2480 His indolence is unplumbed.[13]
2496 Loves warmth, hates work, would live on a radiator.[14]

The worst she could do was to give no report at all, printing the boy's name and number with no comment whatsoever. One of the best, and a very rare one of its kind, read:

2452 A thoroughly capable and efficient, non-talkative boy. What he sets out to do he does well. He is thoroughly British. Twenty shillings to the pound.[15]

It would be interesting to discover what became of George Hannent, whose report this was, and whose bearing and deeds won from Beatie such rare and fulsome praise.

If the magazines were revealing about the boys, they also revealed quite a lot about the editor and her view of life. A Nietzschean footnote in December 1921 reads 'Force, will, and love are the conquerors',[16] while on the opposite page she says, 'Boxing we have done a great deal more at with quite useful results. It is interesting to see boys beaten but hanging on – it is good for them.'

Boxing took place on one night a week, and often included a 'punishment' fight in which two boys entered the ring grossly mismatched. The one destined to lose had somehow offended the woman in command. There was no charge sheet, no appeal against the sentence passed on him: that he should enter the ring with someone heavier, stronger and much more experienced than himself. All the earlier bouts had been watched with enjoyment. Contestants shook hands after the last bell and shrugged off bloody noses, cuts and bruises. The punishment fight was watched in stony silence.

The bell went for the first round, and the battering began. With no hesitation, without any prompting from the referee, whose impartiality was now suspended, the stronger and more experienced fighter tore into his opponent and hammered him round the ring. Very soon the loser was covered in blood. The clock no longer ruled the rounds. They continued until it was deemed that sufficient injury had been done.

After that any trace of enjoyment of the evening vanished. There remained the dry fear of wondering whose turn it would be next, which of them, for reasons never explained, would end up in the loser's corner. Two boys, perfectly good friends and with no grudges, could be pitched against one another, and should the stronger of the two fail to make a convincing show of beating the other senseless he would be back in the ring himself the next boxing night, this time matched with someone less charitably disposed. Only one boy was safe, the most powerful and brutal of their company. Beatie watched the worst blood bath without a trace of dismay, and showed no pity for the most cruelly beaten loser. She would sit at the ringside shouting, 'Make him bleed, boy! Make him bleed!'

Only once did this method of keeping control of the boys go awry. A new boy did well in his first bout and was put in the ring soon after with the expectation that he would thrash a weaker opponent.

He asserted his superiority, but then toyed with his opponent, thinking it unsporting to hurt him more than was necessary to establish himself as the winner. Beatie was furious and had him matched with the ship's bruiser the following week, someone far heavier and far stronger. The new boy took him apart, boxing with extraordinary skill. Round after round he went, mercilessly punishing him, hardly taking a blow in return. Unknown to everybody he had belonged to a boxing club from the age of nine where he had been trained by professionals and could beat almost anyone in a straight fight who had not been similarly trained. He joined the Royal Navy, became Four Fleets champion at his weight – in effect the supreme champion – and turned professional when he came ashore. However, he quit while he was ahead and became an accountant.

In stark contrast to her ringside persona Beatie could write in the magazine of her dismay at human weakness and man's inability to leave the earth and 'get up into the sky' – a feat she said she regularly achieved with the help of 'the Right Pilot'. It was the practical mystic at work again, with a Cromwellian penchant for tough basic decisions made with the assurance of one who claimed to be in direct communication with God.

There was a wistful note in the magazine dated October 1926: 'Every one of our *Mercury* boys on joining the Royal Navy most surely is put on a useful job, but the news or the thanks never reaches us.'[17]

It had simply not occurred to her that her struggle, whether for perfection in the boys or to keep viable the only organisation that gave her freedom and satisfaction, might not always be appreciated.

'Sharkey' Ward departed in December 1923, but it took a while for the shadow he cast to recede, and even when the number of boys who had passed through the ranks had reached 3,500, only about 200 of them remained in regular touch with the ship by letter. A few more returned out of sheer curiosity to look with adult eyes, free at last from fear, on the place that had had such a profound effect on their lives. Beatie had done little to endear herself to them, being as harsh as any chief petty officer or the most hardened regimental sergeant major in the land. When boys arrived back at the beginning of term she had them paraded and looked at them with scorn for having grown their hair and 'gone soft' over the holidays. She walked up and down their ranks and in her deep languid drawl told them what she thought of them and that they would soon be back the way she wanted them, tough, fast, alert and utterly obedient. Even in 1945 when age had reduced her physical stature so that she resembled, as a boy of that year put it, a cartoon grandma, she still retained her awesome personality.

Captain R.E. Hutchins, who was joint captain of Britain's last battleship, HMS *Vanguard* – battleships carried two captains in case one fell ill – and previously captain of the cruiser HMS *Tiger*, began his sea career on the *Mercury* in 1923, just in time to see the last of 'Sharkey' Ward. He was on board for five years, and witnessed a transition from a penal regime to something more acceptable to the world outside. He was three months short of his twelfth birthday when he arrived in Hamble. His brother who came with him was only eight. Their mother had died that year and their father, faced with the responsibility of bringing up seven sons, was glad to get two of them into boarding school.

Hutchins was never in any doubt that Beatie was the sole captain of the ship, with her daughters as able lieutenants. In his account of life on board he describes Beatie as 'deeply religious, kindly and strict'. He continues:

She personally organized the work of the school outside the classrooms, determining routines and writing out work lists in her bold hand. The standards demanded and achieved in dining hall and other buildings, including the chapel, were quite exceptional, and unequalled in anything I have met at sea or elsewhere.[18]

He was unimpressed with the academic standards. The curriculum was massively deficient in the subjects not immediately relevant to the business of turning boys into sailors. Thus his eight-year-old brother, unusually young to be at such a place, missed out on fundamental subjects such as English literature, history, geography, the sciences and a foreign language – subjects which older entrants would at least have had a smattering of before they joined, but would get no more of once through the gates on Satchell Lane.

Another result of this deficiency, though not touched on by Hutchins, was the crippling effect on boys who discovered that life at sea, when they encountered the real thing, was not for them. The gaps in their education left them so short of skills that might enable them to find other forms of employment that some stayed on in an occupation that they found disagreeable, but from which there seemed no escape. There is no mention of Beatie stepping into a classroom, and C.B., the scholar, was seldom there to monitor things. Boys destined for the Merchant Navy, the only ones of the company who fully expected to become ships' officers, were singularly deprived since they spent longer on the ship than the rest. They were exposed to only one teacher, much as they had been at Junior School between the ages of seven and eleven.

From the mid-1920s to the early 1950s this was a man who had never qualified as a navigator, yet purported to teach the subject. There were no charts, chart instruments or sextant, no azimuth mirror resting on a binnacle outdoors to practise taking bearings, no chronometer, tide tables, pilot books nor any of the literature of their subject. The rules for the prevention of collisions at sea – the absolute fundamentals of their calling – were never taught. Instead, his classes learned parrot-fashion a few navigational formulae and at the end of the school year duly received marks out of 100 for a subject of which they had only the barest inkling. Another deficiency was in the matter of signals. They had no training in the skill beyond seeing the Morse code for individual letters of the alphabet written up on a blackboard, one letter a day. In the Merchant Navy, to which boys in this class were headed, the deck officer on watch is his own signalman.

For those destined to join the RN there were no deficiencies. Hutchins's own experience as a senior naval officer suggested that, apart from sea-going experience, standards on the *Mercury* were comparable to those required for petty officers in the Royal Navy. Divisional Officers in RN entry establishments almost fought to get *Mercury* boys into their divisions when a new batch arrived, so useful were they in helping with the process of turning raw recruits into disciplined people like themselves. In many cases these men were alumni of the *Mercury* and knew better than anybody what to expect of them.

That Captain Hutchins in retirement could speak of Beatie as a kindly woman gave another insight into her character. Most of her kindnesses, however, had to be concealed for fear they might detract from her commanding image. Boys came from every social class, some from broken homes, whose fees were paid by charities, who had nowhere to go for their holidays. One of them, Leonard Casimir, was the son of a stationmaster who had died leaving him to be cared for by unsympathetic relatives who could not wait to get rid of him. In his first term at the *Mercury* in 1928 a boy died of pneumonia and the grieving parents, housekeepers to Sir Arthur Conan Doyle, creator of Sherlock Holmes, asked to be allowed to have a homeless boy come to them for the holidays. Beatie, a friend of the author, chose Leonard from the group in need, a sensitive, intelligent and well-mannered boy who would cope in the unusual surroundings into which he was about to be dropped. Leonard stayed in two of the author's houses, one in the heart of the New Forest and the other near Crowborough in Sussex. He dined at Sir Arthur's table and attended his seances in one of which the medium said the boy's father was present and described him in perfect detail. When Sir Arthur died in 1930 Leonard was sent with other homeless boys to stay on a farm in the Cotswolds, again organised by Beatie. They took their hammocks with them, slept in the attic, worked on the farm for sixpence a day and enjoyed themselves immensely.[19]

As time went on a few boys – Hutchins was the most notable – exhibited to such an outstanding extent the approved qualities of leadership, toughness and so forth, that she softened, slightly at least, in their direction. They had become instruments of her rule, and left to their own devices they would exact the same high standards from those around them. In Hutchins's case high intelligence was added to all-round capability. In December 1927 he took nearly a quarter of the awards on Prize Day. HRH the Prince of Wales, who had been invited to hand out the prizes, suggested to him that he stay close at hand since Hutchins could barely get back to his seat before his number was called again.

If Hutchins represented the standards Beatie was striving to attain at the *Mercury*, the visit of the Prince of Wales represented a further stage in her rehabilitation into the society from which she had been excluded by the events of her youth.

ELEVEN

Half Greek, Half Malvolio!

The 1920s were both the worst and the best years of Beatie's rule. In the early part of the decade her authority was so pitiless that half a century later men who had suffered it spoke of her as hard, mean, cruel, sadistic, unfeeling, unwomanly – one said that 'no normal woman could be so insensitive'. Such praise as she elicited was of the most grudging kind. She taught them sailing in cutters and whalers, and was clearly a better sailor than some of them would ever be. There were still tenders attached to the ship, such as the *Vishala*, a converted fishing craft, and Beatie would sometimes skipper one of these on a trip well out into the Solent. A favourite destination was Alum Bay on the Isle of Wight. If there was a good sea running many of the boys were seasick, but not Beatie. (Those who were not sick dined well, having commandeered the packed luncheons of those who were.) But the descriptions of her from the mid-1920s onwards are less bitter, though without exception her ability to strike fear into everybody is still mentioned with awe. By this time she seemed to have gained all the respect she was ever likely to require.

The trickle of ex-*Mercury* boys proceeding to commissions in the armed forces rose steadily, and even those who were not officer material invariably gave a good account of themselves. Many of them came from prosperous educated families and would undoubtedly have achieved high rank even without Beatie's so-called 'scientific system of character training' as advertised in a prospectus dated 1926. Most who went into the Royal Navy, however, acknowledged a debt to her for having set them on their careers with qualities of speed and resilience that placed them ahead of their competitors. As was to be expected, Merchant Navy entrants became officers, but here again there was success beyond expectations. More than one of the great Cunarders had an ex-*Mercury* in command.

Beatie had also achieved more than enough respectability. The visit by the Prince of Wales was followed two years later by one from the Duke of York, the prince's brother and later King George VI. The official timetable for the visit ('11.30. His Royal Highness leaves Waterloo Station by train') was preceded by a list of those who held honorary offices in the governing body of the ship. It read:

President:
The Lord Bishop of Winchester
Vice-Presidents:
Admiral C.S. Hickley, CB, MVO
The Rt Hon. The Earl of Birkenhead
Lord Apsley, DSO, MC
Lord Riddell
Montagu Rendall, Esq. LLD
Lord Louis Mountbatten
The Rt Hon. Lord Lee of Fareham, GCSI etc.
Captain Basil Lubbock
The Rt Hon. Sir John Simon, KCVO, etc.
Professor Seward, SCD (Camb.), FRS
A.J. Spender, Esq.
Rear-Admiral C. Tibbitts, CBE, MVO, etc.
H.E. The Hon. Sir F. Stanley Jackson
The Hon. Mr Justice Roache
Rear-Admiral B.G. Thesiger, CB, etc.[1]

Undoubtedly the friendships of C.B.'s time at Oxford brought some of them on board, but it was not enough to explain so much greatness, so many accomplished figures ready to associate themselves with a tiny nautical school in Hampshire. Half of their number would have looked well on the headed notepaper of the richest private-sector school. It had to be Beatie's connections in high places and the fact that she had made the *Mercury* the best in its class, that of privately owned nautical schools. If it was the best in England, then it was one of the best in the world, and the great names merely added distinction to distinction.

There was, however, just the vague suspicion that people were still shy of being associated too closely with Beatie. In January 1979 Admiral of the Fleet the Earl Mountbatten of Burma, writing of his link with the ship when he was its president in its closing years, long after Beatie and C.B. had gone, remarked, 'We all heard stories about how she [Beatie] ran the *Mercury* on a very taut discipline and she was respected, but also feared.'[2] What Mountbatten did not mention was that his connection pre-dated his presidency by many years, that he had been a vice-president in the 1920s, and he had not just 'heard stories'. Only after his tragic death in 1979 did this come to light, with evidence that he and his wife had often visited the ship when Beatie was running it. Nor had events surrounding the origins of the *Mercury* been forgotten even in the 1930s. Professor Sir Geoffrey Callender of the Royal Naval College, Greenwich wrote to Sir James Caird in February 1930 on the subject of Charles Hoare's collection of ship models and naval artefacts that Sir James had acquired for the maritime museum in Greenwich. Callender spoke in his letter of a visit to the college by 'our friend Schweder [who] brought with him [Lord] Arthur Somerset':

I showed the two of them the Mercury models and other treasures. Somerset, who is a man of seventy-four, knew Hoare very well and filled up several gaps in our knowledge of his career. Somerset said that the lady [Beatie] broke her leg in the hunting field when Hoare was Master of the Vale of White Horse, [and] stayed in Hoare's house so long that two things happened; one, Mrs. Hoare left her husband, and two, the surrounding country declined to allow Hoare to draw their covers. He was in consequence compelled to give up the pack, and it was then that he took up the Training Ship Mercury. Somerset also added that

Hoare and the lady had several children but here the chronicle becomes almost too scandalous to put on paper.

He concluded with the words: 'Poor Beatrice.'[3]

Although Lord Somerset was mistaken in some of his details – Beatie did not break her leg, nor did Mrs Hoare leave her husband altogether until four years after the 'accident' in the hunting field – it is clear that the Gloucestershire Scandal was remembered and discussed, and not with any particular affection.

The 1920s gave way to the 1930s with Beatie still in command, and her daughters still assisting her. The new decade began with a new building, the recreation hall having been destroyed by fire. The brick structure that went up in its stead was subsequently referred to as the 'New Place' and had a figure of the god Mercury poised on the roof. Inside were panelled walls and murals painted by Gregory Robinson, the distinguished marine artist.

For the remaining years of Beatie's life only minor changes took place in the daily routine. Some of the more futile punishments disappeared as the men who had devised them reached retirement. The beatings ceased after a boy emerged from one with blood running down the backs of his legs – and ran home on the same day. The boy's parents took the man responsible to court, but he was found not guilty. In the dining-hall wooden bowls and spoons had given way to normal dishes and cutlery – a mixed blessing to the boys, one of whose duties was to clean and polish every item as if their lives depended on it.

Throughout the 1920s and 1930s C.B. Fry was absent for long spells, but though his appearances on the site at Hamble were brief, the impression he made was never less than striking. Walker, who was comforted by him when life was becoming unbearable, tells of his arriving on the playing field unexpectedly when boys were playing cricket.

He took the bat from one of the boys and showed how it should be held. Then he gave us a display of his agility. He sent a boy to get a chair. When it was fetched Cdr. Fry stood behind it, his feet flexed.

'Now you should all be able to do this,' he said to the little crowd that had collected.

He suddenly went down so that he was nearly sitting on his heels. Then he shot up into the air and landed in front of the chair, bolt upright and with both feet still together. It was a marvellous display of agility – and showmanship.[4]

C.B. was then forty-eight. In his mid-fifties he was demonstrating athletics, 'floating over the hurdles', as one witness put it.

Mobsby – he who had taken a sixpence or two off C.B. in the nets – described him at one of his more relaxed pastimes:

Any boy who had business in the playing field in the early morning would often see C.B. in pyjamas and ornate dressing gown, sitting on one of the wooden seats which surrounded it, fishing rod in hand, casting a fly on to a postcard lying on the grass about twenty to thirty feet away.[5]

This was the picture presented by most accounts of C.B. on the ship: eccentric – what normal commanding officer would be caught practising fly-fishing in his pyjamas? – and showing off a little, but generally detached from the day-to-day slog of the place. E.W. Swanton remarked in his book, *Sort of a Cricketing Person*, that 'Nothing was undersize about Charles [Fry]',[6] and added, 'least of all his kindness to the young'. It was an aspect of his character he seldom showed in a place dedicated to Spartan living, but at least his presence was un-menacing and his image as a noble man unspoilt. On the rare occasion when he interfered in the running of the ship it was still in keeping with his image. When he saw a boy being bullied, he took him aside and arranged for him to have an intensive course in boxing. It was not a 'Sharkey' Ward course. He was taught to duck, weave, think fast, and hit without getting hit too often in return. Satisfied that the difference in the abilities between bullied and bully had been narrowed, he put them in the ring together and saw his protégé turn the tables so effectively that the loser started to fight foul, kicking and hitting below the belt. C.B. had a riding crop handy and beat him soundly, probably the only occasion he ever struck a boy, but one which was unmistakably just.

In the village of Hamble the same impression prevailed – of a man who was pleasantly eccentric, kind, but rather remote, too taken up with his affairs in places as far afield as London, Geneva and India to be concerned with local matters.

The busy life elsewhere was perhaps too busy. The League of Nations met in Geneva in 1920 with C.B. as an acting substitute Delegate of the Indian representation, writing speeches for K.S. Ranjitsinhji. Back in England the following year, he made the first of three unsuccessful attempts to get into Parliament, standing for the Liberals at Brighton. The same year, he travelled to India in time for the 1921–2 visit by the Prince of Wales. A year later it was politics again, fighting Banbury for the Liberals. Back at the League of Nations in 1923, he wrote the speech delivered by Ranjitsinhji that probably checked Mussolini's ambitions in the Adriatic after he had sent ships to bombard and occupy Corfu. While still at Geneva there occurred that strange episode when a bishop from Albania was authorised to find 'an English country gentleman with ten thousand a year' to become King of Albania, the throne being vacant. Ranjitsinhji handled the negotiations; C.B. was actually interviewed by the bishop, but nothing came of it. (To *Mercury* boys, had they heard of this, the prospect of C.B. as king of that country would have been less intriguing than that of his wife as his Queen and Consort, and what this might do to the Albanians.)

C.B. made his third and final attempt to gain a seat in Parliament in 1924, when he stood at Oxford. His defeat did not mean the end of his busy life outside the *Mercury*, however. His acquaintance with powerful, wealthy and talented people took him to all parts of the country and to India.

Whether it was the furious pace of his life or some dark incident in the course of a visit to India which brought on the bout of mental illness that overwhelmed C.B. for several years is impossible to decide with any accuracy. His behaviour was bizarre – he was said to have run naked along Brighton beach, and at home he hugged his possessions in fear of their being stolen by imaginary thieves. For the first few years of the 1930s he had to be looked after by a nurse, often staying at a house in Maidenhead made available to him by Ranjitsinhji. Ironically, C.B. could not bear to see his benefactor, as a curious manifestation of his illness was a horror of Indian people. There were times when he was lucid and in possession of all his faculties, and then he would be taken to visit the homes of sympathetic friends. He could discuss his symptoms with them. The Begbie family, at whose house he was always welcome, listened to him as he described his feelings when emerging from a passage of the illness in its most extreme form. For a while as he surfaced he was apparently beyond communication, neither responding to the people about him nor offering any sign of what he was feeling or thinking, but he assured the Begbies that he was fully aware of what was happening. He told them how he had been to a house for tea, the chauffeur, who also acted as a nurse, taking him in the Bentley. His host poured boiling water into the teapot without first putting in the tea-leaves. C.B. saw the error and did nothing, then watched the confusion, still without comment or the slightest reaction, as clear water was poured into the cups.

During one of his lucid spells he was invited to a house in the New Forest to meet the Headmaster of Picket Post School, Frank Andrews. Like C.B., Andrews had graduated in classics at Oxford, and the two men sat at opposite ends of a first-floor balcony overlooking the forest and declaimed Greek verse to each other. Joan Begbie was there at the time. For her the delight C.B. showed on this occasion was a clue to his condition. As the evening wore on he shed his years and the burden of his illness and became young and vital again, the Greek god of Wadham, at one with the heroes in the verses he shouted into the night. For years his life had swung between the poles of a frantic public life and the rigidly governed affairs of the *Mercury*, affairs in which he had very little say.

At neither pole did he find a response as refreshing as that to be had from a fellow classics scholar.

When Beatie was asked what had brought on her husband's illness she replied 'Thwarted genius.'[7] It was a revealing reply; it told the questioner as much about Beatie as it did about her husband. She treated him with compassion throughout the whole period of his illness, and there is little to suggest that the domineering manner, which characterised her dealings with the boys on the ship, had helped to bring it about; but her own lack of education, her inability to respond to her husband in an area and on a theme which was crucial to his life, may have been a contributory factor.

The four-year duration confirmed her captaincy of the *Mercury*, supposing there were any who doubted who was really in charge. There was a glimpse of her financial independence when she bought another Rolls-Royce in 1930, a 1925 Phantom 1 belonging to the Prince of Wales, who was buying a newer model. She paid £1,700 for it, with her old Roller taken in part exchange.[8]

C.B.'s illness receded in 1934, and he attended his only son's wedding to Yvonne Blunt of New Jersey. The caption to a newspaper photograph, taken outside a London registry office, read, 'Mr Fry (C.B.) who is 62, has, to the great joy of his army of friends, made a complete recovery after a serious health breakdown.'[9]

The 'health breakdown' is examined by Dr Peter Toghill, FRCP, and the psychiatrist Dr J. Waite in an article in the 1999 edition of the *Journal of Medical Biography*. They note C.B.'s disastrous final year at Oxford, with only a fourth class in *literae humaniores*. There are suggestions of alcoholism, a near-collapse in 1924 under the pressures of the unsuccessful bid to enter Parliament and the furious pace of his life generally. The doctors diagnosed a bipolar affective disorder, something that may have explained why this prodigiously gifted man achieved relatively little off the sports field in later life.[10]

There were five more years in the public eye before C.B. slipped into the shadows, with only one or two glimpses thereafter before his death in 1956. He travelled in Germany in 1934 and continued his work at home as a sports correspondent. In this capacity he left for a round-the-world tour late in 1936 in the company of Neville Cardus, who was sure that, if he had put his mind to it, C.B. could have won the highest honours in half-a-dozen lofty walks of life. 'He walked the field half Greek, half Malvolio', was another phrase Cardus used to describe him, invoking at once the fickle gods of ancient legend and the giddy poseur of *Twelfth Night* in an attempt to pin down the elusive qualities of this strange man. Writing of their voyage together, Cardus told how C.B. held court among the deck-chairs on the *Orion* as she ploughed patiently through the seas:

> He dressed differently every day; sometimes with topee and short leather trousers as though about to trace the source of the Amazon; or in a scaled green sort of costume which made him look like a deep-sea monster; or in a bath towel, worn like a toga. One day, to tease him, I said, 'Good morning, Charles. No hemlock yet? Give us your ideas about the Iambic.' In full spate came forth a swift survey of the origin and development of the Iambic, with quotations from all periods and writers, every sentence ending with 'You see what I mean' or 'However'. A sort of intellectual Jack Bunsby; an original and fascinating man.[11]

It was inevitable that a man of such extraordinary character and intellect, with such a varied career to look back on and a considerable flair for words, should write his autobiography. It was published in October 1939, much of it having been dictated to his friend, Denzil Batchelor. In his own book about C.B., Batchelor records his amazement at the ease with which the lines were delivered, page after page filling up with rarely a pause for alterations. All the sport was there, the cricket, the athletics, Rugby and soccer – his joy in the latter sometimes showing through even more than in his first love, cricket. Every chapter glitters with famous names, so many that they make up the greater part of a nine-page closely printed index – sportsmen, scholars, writers, artists, princes and maharajahs, earls and actresses, all of them met on equal terms, and attracting the same kind of lively anecdotes.

TWELVE

Reaching Home

The war years, 1939–45, were the last in which the *Mercury* management could fairly claim that their system of training was suited to the demands of the Royal Navy. The business of the *Mercury* was war, and such refinements as a library or a science lab did not exist in a place devoted quite properly, as was felt, to producing the kind of recruits the Navy wanted. On Prize Day there were nine prizes for school subjects, including Divinity, Reading and Recitation, but there were the same number of prizes awarded for 'Qualities', such as 'Initiative', 'Cheerful Obedience', 'Perseverance', and 'Unselfishness and Good Humour', all of which reinforced the quality that lay at the heart of their training – the ability to offer blind obedience to whoever was in charge, and, in time, to move up the ladder of authority and expect the same attitudes from those below them. They were highly disciplined, these *Mercury* boys, but in 1945 a handful of men had flown to the skies over Hiroshima and Nagasaki and destroyed both cities, and in a few seconds had called into question the concept of discipline as it was understood on the *Mercury*. The great navies of the world had been rendered obsolete at a stroke and new forms of excellence, new disciplines, were suddenly in demand that were not catered for at the *Mercury*.

If the rank-and-file could not recognise these changes, it was to be hoped that their immediate superiors could, but their precarious tenure, holding office only as long as they too gave blind obedience to the woman in command, ruled out the possibility of change, while she, for her part, showed no sign of losing her grip on the place. Week after week they saw her appear, moving slowly as became her eighty-three years, but sturdily. If they sought signs of weakening powers in her voice or expression there were none to record. Sybil was her eyes and ears in the places she could not reach on her own, and her rule was absolute. Her son and her daughters Charis and Faith had left, the daughters escaping at last to join the Women's Royal Naval Service – the 'Wrens' – where, by this time, they had become Chief Officers, the equivalent of Commanders in the RN, but their departure had altered nothing.

How long could this last? At some point Beatie had to be told that she had gone on too long. Or would the end come in another way, from the reluctance of parents to send their sons to a school so obviously out of touch with the times? Already there was a suspicion that people in local governments up and down the country with scholarships to dispense were sending 'problem' boys instead of grammar school material, boys who were 'in need of discipline'. There were boys from expensive preparatory schools in the ranks, one at least of whom had been misled into thinking that he was going to attend 'the Eton of the south', and though they were in the minority, they represented the type of youth that had been the backbone of the place for years, sons of people who set a high value on the boarding school that offered a rugged outdoor life as part of the educational experience, and also one that, for all the deficiencies of its curriculum, still carried the aura of C.B. Fry. Such boys now found that they had strange companions, like the one who at first amused his watch by stealing all the bootlaces of a neighbouring watch, and then shocked them by stealing all theirs as well. He went on to loot their hiding-places of stamps, envelopes, writing paper and money, the very things they had stored away in defiance of all attempts to stop them getting letters through to the outside world. Not even being flung into the mud of the Hamble at low tide checked him; it seemed that he was not alone, that there were others like him scattered through the sections, the type who had not been welcome even in the days when Charles Hoare was looking for recruits in the poorer parts of London.

I was one of those who expected the *Mercury* to be a rather more glamorous kind of boarding school. I write of the final months of

Beatie's rule with the vivid recollection of one who was there.

In the autumn of 1945 an evening of boxing came to an end with Boy No. 3488 Crabtree cast as executioner in a punishment fight. Mr Fraser presided over bell and stopwatch. When the bell went for the first round Crabtree dutifully tore into his opponent in full knowledge that there was at least one beefy oaf at the ringside who would do the same to him a week later if he hesitated. In no time at all he reduced his opponent to a bloody shambles. The obsession with cleanliness on the *Mercury* did not extend to the canvas on which they fought. It was brown with the spilt blood of hundreds of fights, and now it was showered with more bright specks that would dry and blend with the rest. A right from Crabtree, and his opponent's head snapped back, and the scarlet spray scattered as far as the benches lining the ringside. The first round went on far too long, and the contestants had barely sat down when the bell went for the second. Crabtree came forward, punched hard, and then held back as fresh blood ran from his opponent's face. For a few moments they prodded each other, the predictable winner feeling he had done enough damage for one evening, and the loser relieved that the barrage of hard blows had ceased. Suddenly there was a roar from the ringside. Fraser was halfway to his feet and shouting in frightened rage: 'Get in there and beat him! If you don't I'll come in and beat both of you myself.'

Crabtree resumed the punishment, but the instigator of this fight was sitting in her living-room poring over the details of the work done that day and preparing for the next. With only a few months to live she seemed unaware of any alternative to her stance of decades, setting men and boys at each other's throats, demanding, bullying, driving, never letting up in the pursuit of what she saw as her duty. And there was no alternative while individuals and nations felt compelled to compete rather than to cooperate. She seemed to personify not only the waste of women's capabilities, but those of all humanity.

The winter of 1945/6 was cold and wet. There were gales strong enough to stop the movement of shipping in the Solent, but on the

Hamble the traffic of boats between the pier and the dormitory ship went on uninterrupted. One January morning the rough-weather crew, having put the ship's company ashore, became too exhausted to return the cutter to its moorings and were swept upriver. They landed at Bursledon where early risers were treated to the spectacle of eleven boys in oilskins and sou'westers, barefooted, padding silently along the pavements in the direction of Hamble village.

The Easter holidays in April were approaching when Beatie attended Saturday Divisions for the last time. She had stopped in the middle of her inspection and, for the first time in the memory of most of those present, addressed the whole gathering: 'I wish you would not call each other by your numbers. I wish you would call each other by your names. Numbers are so insensitive.'

There was not a flicker of reaction from the two lines of boys facing each other as usual across the narrow strip of tarmac. There were still many items to be held up for her to see and only when she went back to her rooms would we feel safe. Fraser was at her elbow, anxious as ever, ready to record the faults she was bound to find no matter how diligently people, men and boys alike, tried to get it right. She was not above poking a boy with her stick and commenting on his character with words that would stay with him for ever: 'You have a shiny seat to your trousers. That's the only part of you that will shine for the rest of your life', or she might hint that he was due in the boxing ring as he needed taking down a peg or two. But on this day she seemed to sail past us, barely looking at the garments held out for her to see. When the inspection was over she spoke again before leaving us, her face radiant: 'There are going to be lots of changes, aren't there Mr. Fraser.'

This was delivered as a statement, not as a question. His expression when he heard it, one of relief that the business of the morning was nearly over, turned to one of bleak misgiving that bordered on terror.

Six days later Mrs Fry fell and broke her hip. She stayed in her own bedroom for three days, during which time all bugle calls ceased and orders were given softly so that she might not be disturbed. Boots, which in any case were worn only for drill, were left in their lockers. On 15 April she was taken to the RSH Infirmary, Southampton, where little Geoffrey Petch had stopped on his way home to a grave on the banks of the Humber.

It was Wednesday of that week when McGavin assembled the ship's company in the chapel. He bade us kneel and bow our heads. There was a long pause before he could bring himself to speak. He was a tall man, with the erect carriage of one who had been in the band of the Grenadier Guards. He was handsome, with strong black hair swept back from a pale, lean, slightly ascetic face. I looked up and saw that this face was white with anguish, and that he was close to tears. At last he began: 'The time has come to tell you that there is no hope for Mrs. Fry.'

He went on to tell of a life of dedication, over half a century devoted utterly to the establishment of which we were a part. He did not reveal the extraordinary circumstances that had set her on this course. Perhaps he did not know of them.

In addition to the anguish at the prospect of Beatie's death McGavin must have felt great anxiety about his own future. Beatie may have needed the continuity he represented, someone with whom she could confer about the running and the future of the ship as she had done with his father. Fraser was a loyal servant who feared her; the late James McGavin was a loyal friend on whom she bestowed her affection. His son proved a worthy successor, sustaining the musical and religious values that were so important to her.

We left the ship for the Easter holiday and returned a fortnight later to learn that Beatie had reached Home on 23 April, and had been cremated. In her will she asked – enigmatically – for her ashes to 'be scattered in the air'. In fact they were scattered on the rose gardens which she had planted overlooking the River Hamble.

A few weeks later, the priest who had given her the last rites of the Church, was officiating at a communion service in the chapel, attended by a few boys who came to the altar rail to receive the bread and wine. One of them asked afterwards why communion had not been given to the old lady kneeling beside him. There was nobody there. He had been next to the place where Beatie had always knelt when she took wine and wafer.

No tears were shed for Beatie, at least not among the boys she had ruled. The local newspaper assured its readers – in case there should have been any doubt – that *Mercury* boys had loved her.[1] A few may have felt that way – Eric McGavin, perhaps, who had grown up in the shadow of the *Mercury*, had trained there and had then returned as an adult with privileged access to The House and so to another side of Beatie's character. The rest regarded her with awe, pity, admiration, loathing, fear, respect – a whole range of emotions – but certainly not love. Boys had always been known to her by their numbers, even the few to whom she had given nicknames, and it was difficult to feel love for a person who ruled your life with a rod of iron and treated you as a cipher. Too late she had appealed to us to use each other's names, and told us what we already knew – that numbers were 'insensitive'.

The new term began with a whiff of change. Would Sybil Hoare assume the role of her mother and inspect us on Saturday mornings? She did not, but continued examining our work, the cleaning, polishing, and scrubbing we had done, while Fraser conducted the ceremonies at the veranda exactly as if Beatie had been there.

The only dramatic change was in Sybil's appearance. She was dressed from head to toe in new clothes; her hair, which had always been pulled back and tied up in a bun, was more informally arranged and one could see that it had a natural curl. She seemed more approachable and even attempted a smile and a few pleasantries in her dealings with us. Immature and lacking any insight into the nature of her relationship with her mother, we could not see the changed appearance and attitudes for what they probably were, celebrations of her release from decades of subservience. For years this woman of illustrious descent had inspected everything on behalf of her mother, including the bucket lavatories. Equally celebratory, perhaps, was the bonfire Sybil made of the mass of papers and photographs that had been cleared out of her mother's rooms. Documents invaluable to future biographers and historians went up in smoke, destroyed by the living who wished to close doors on the past. In this case, however, it is very likely that the dead also wanted the past forgotten. Beatie, aware that her life had run on more than ordinary lines, indicated to Fraser that she did not want her story told. Loyal servant that he was, he kept her secrets, and turned away many who came to him for help, believing, quite rightly, that there was a gripping tale to be told about how a woman came to be in charge of a nautical school for boys, but unable to get at the roots of the story. He may, in fact, have known very little about her, no more perhaps than the garbled account given by Lord Arthur Somerset to Sir Geoffrey Callender, but even this he kept to himself in loyalty to Beatie.

High-ranking officers of the armed forces, including Admiral of the Fleet Sir James Somerville, were at Beatie's memorial service on 22 May, the thirty-eighth anniversary of the death of her lover, Charles Hoare. The tiny chapel was made to accommodate 400 people, many of them from the great training establishments of the Royal Navy who knew first hand what wonders were wrought when a new batch of *Mercury* boys appeared at their gates. The only boys present were in the choir. I was one of them.

Two priests conducted the service, the *Mercury* chaplain, the Revd Dr Machin and the Revd A.E. Pavey, Vicar of Hamble, representing the Bishop of Winchester. The Revd A.L.E. Hoskyns-Abrahall who had known Beatie for years gave the address. As a former naval officer, now a priest, he had been tipped as a possible successor to C.B. when the time came for him to retire as Captain Superintendent. He described her as a genius, but added that her genius was not some gift that made it easier for her to do her work than other people. 'It was rather', he went on, 'that classical definition of genius, an infinite capacity for taking pains.' No doubt he thought he had paid further tribute to her when he remarked that 'She went on where lesser men would have stopped satisfied.'

It was a sentence that unwittingly embraced the whole triumph and tragedy of her life. If a man had achieved as much there would have been no memorial service, no gathering of admirals and other officers to honour his memory, since he would have achieved no more than was expected of him. But a woman had done this, and, while it was unquestionably a triumph for her, it was also a tragedy, for, if the assembly had thought about it at all, they would have found it monstrous that there were regiments of women, armies of them, perhaps, with as much courage, staying power and fortitude – and certainly with far greater intellects than the woman they were honouring – yet with little or no recognition of their powers, singly or collectively, nor adequate space in which to exercise them. The constraints of her early life had left her with only her strength of character as the means to success, which may have explained why so many of the prizes awarded on the ship each year went to boys who displayed similar qualities. Lacking formal education she was accustomed to say that inspiration was better than information. For the uninformed this might be sufficient, but the discriminating prefer an inspired performance from actors who know their lines. None, however, doubted her ability to command in spite of these deficiencies.

In the *Mercury Magazine* of March 1927, a footnote reads, 'A great ship asks deep waters.' Beatrice Holme Fry was like a great ship rammed hard aground in the shallows of the Hamble. Nevertheless, she fought for over half a century to make, then to keep, a foothold in the world worthy of her extraordinary talent, that of moulding the lives of others to her own standards. In the *Mercury*'s core subject of discipline of the martial kind those standards were high. It was her fate that she should work among men in that hitherto most manly of occupations, seafaring. Generations of *Mercury* boys paid dearly in order that she might succeed against all the odds, but at least they entered the services so highly trained that most won immediate advancement. No one should be allowed to think for a moment that a woman would demand less of those around her than a man, and so the rules became stricter and the expectations higher than they had been under Charles Hoare. It was no surprise to anyone on the premises that all hands could be mustered for inspection by Winston

Churchill in less than ten minutes. The place was always ready for inspection, but the visitor did not get to see the effort required to maintain this level of preparedness. They did not see Reid's brutal game of 'luffs and tackles', the dreary file of barefoot boys jogging by the hour round the signal mast, the occasional figure shivering for hours at the cross-trees of the same mast, the terrified boy tied hand and foot to the gun for a flogging, the crumpled figure on the grass of the sports field when a 'shake-up' had gone on too long. Before the school broke up for Christmas and on other special occasions the gallery of the theatre was crowded with guests who listened in rapture – often in tears – to the music welling up from the auditorium as the ship's company sang to them in performances that took months to rehearse. This was discipline of another kind and the pride of those who answered to it must not be discounted, but to some it was too dearly bought.

Even in death Beatie remained formidable. In her will she trusts that the *Mercury* will be carried on 'as a work our country needs'. Stephen gets no mention. She had ignored his marriage to Yvonne Blunt, and it was only after his mother's death that he returned home with his wife and sons. Sybil gets a string of pearls, but only for use in her lifetime and then to be passed on to Charis or Faith. Investments and property are shared equally between Charis and Faith. She urges her children to 'settle down and work without regard to the insignificance of their task, whatever it may be', a remark that seems to admit that in denying them freedom and formal education she had left them unprepared for work of significance. She senses the possibility of a gulf between her children born to C.B. and those born to Charles Hoare when she asks them to be 'kind and generous' to Faith. She pleads with the Hoare children 'especially [to] protect and care for Faith . . . whether she should desire such protection or not', words that suggest a waywardness observed in one who in all probability was struggling to free herself into a world for which she was totally unprepared. The sting is in the tail. Charis, if she marries a certain William Loveday, is to be disinherited 'as if my said daughter were dead'.

For all that she had fought so long and hard, it is not enough to ascribe her tough stance entirely to the need to succeed in a man's world. There was the struggle – successful as it turned out – for recognition by the aristocracy who had excluded her in the aftermath of the Gloucestershire Scandal. Recognition, however, could not bring back the grandeur of life at Hatchlands, something she may have hoped to recover in her initial and childish infatuation for a rich man, and subsequently in an almost grim attachment to him that went on even after his death, attending his grave and keeping his seat in the chapel decorated with flowers. She was like Tennyson's 'great Princess' – 'grand, epic, homicidal' – but in the end she could find no larger estate in which to be her regal self than the forty-five acres sandwiched between Satchell Lane and the river.

Some saw Beatie's life at the *Mercury* as a long expiation for a decade of youthful folly, and the intense nature of her religious life as an element in this. There was no denying her devotion to the ideal of the crucified Christ, 'The Green Hill King', as she called Him. At almost every Prize Day concert in the Building the Prelude to *Parsifal* was played; the programme notes included the words, 'Only through pain and suffering can peace be won.' She was ready to accept hardship, and she imposed it in cruel measure on those under her command. She was deeply religious, but it seemed to have escaped her that her 'Green Hill King' had preached a doctrine of love. Quite how she could have reconciled the Christian doctrine of love with the harsh necessities of life for a woman running an all-male establishment must remain a dilemma of universal concern, one that makes her life – in the fullest classical sense – a profound tragedy.

Epilogue

If Beatie was a genius to the extent of possessing an infinite capacity for taking pains, her husband was one on a more generous scale. 'The true genius', wrote Samuel Johnson 'is a mind of large general powers accidentally determined to some particular direction.'[1] That C.B. had such powers was universally recognised. As his prowess at sport declined with advancing years, one might have expected that his intellectual gifts would have led to a different, but equally eminent career. Based on the *Mercury*, whether from a sense of duty or from an inability to organise himself to greater purpose, he fell short of his country's expectations. The forays to India and the League of Nations were no substitute for the achievements expected of a man who had shown promise of becoming one of 'the choice and master spirits of his age', and Neville Cardus's description of him as 'the admirable Crichton of games' put the seal on a career over which there must hang more darkly than for most the shadow of what might have been. C.B. may have known this. In the summer of 1946 I came ashore at dawn before the rest of the company to work in the kitchen as galley boy, preparing breakfast. I saw the old man dressed in a greatcoat standing on the slipway of the boathouse. I passed within a few feet of him, but he did not notice me, for he was staring across the river at the dormitory ship with a look on his face as of one who had stumbled on a scene of unspeakable horror. Was I witness, perhaps, to that terrible moment when at last it dawned on him that things might have been different?

After the death of his wife C.B. Fry struggled briefly to keep the *Mercury* unchanged, but he lacked the charisma with which she had

153

held the system whole, bound in a strong chain. When it snapped things fell apart. The charismatics are undemocratic. They do not confer freedom on the people who live in their shadow. Those in the shadow may prefer it that way, finding ease from the burden of decisions.

In 1950 C.B. retired to a flat in Andover Court, a block of flats on the corner of Hendon Way and the Finchley Road in north-west London. Stephen and Yvonne Fry took over a hotel in the New Forest, 12 miles from Southampton. The Master Builder stands on the bank of the River Beaulieu next to the hard from which the great ships of Nelson's day were launched. Sybil Hoare went with them. C.B. visited his family at Beaulieu and residents of the hotel found mementoes of his life as sportsman scattered through the building, photographs on the walls, or his cricket bag left casually on a landing as though he were still about to carry it to Lord's to captain another game against Australia, but gradually the man who had loved an audience become more reclusive, spending most of his time at his flat in London.

There was a brief return to the limelight in 1955 when he was guest of honour on the television programme *This Is Your Life*. The carefully staged pleasantries, the figures from the great man's past previously drilled in what to say, filled out the usual half-hour of television time with the details of an astonishing career. There seemed to be no shadows, no dark corners, to mar the impression that this had indeed been a life worth living.

After C.B.'s death the following year many of his own generation, and the hero-worshipping generation that came after, expressed their regrets that the promise of his early days had not been fulfilled. In the early 1900s his private box at Lord's had overflowed with men who had come to honour him: G.K. Chesterton, Hilaire Belloc, E.V. Lucas, John Drinkwater, Rider Haggard, Clifford and Arnold Bax – men whose works endure where his are barely remembered. In the lives and the autobiographies of the great, the famous and the powerful who dined at his table in Mercury House – Winston Churchill, Baden-Powell, Kipling and many others – there is little or no mention of their meeting with C.B. When he does come to their attention he is hedged about with reservations. Sir Maurice Bowra, Warden of Wadham College from 1938 to 1970, described him as 'eager, and natural . . . though perhaps he lived on a manic curve, of which I never saw the downward trend',[2] while Lord Birkenhead, the 2nd Earl, said of C.B. that the brilliant early promise petered out in after years 'into a somewhat desultory and disappointed career'.[3]

That C.B. in his declining years at the *Mercury* should lie awake at nights reciting aloud the details of the games he had played was a source of dismay to some who knew of this habit. The charitable could have said that it was the sports writer in him recalling the game in order that he might write about it the following day for his newspaper column, but others would be saddened that so much greatness had come to this – reliving former glories in the absence of present acclaim. If one could be permitted to suggest an alternative career it would have been at Oxford. He could have been the glory of his university, classics don, writer, sportsman, in life a glittering presence at the college of his choice who would have brought the finest scholars clamouring to be associated with him, in death a legend that would have grown with every new telling.

C.B. died in London on 7 September 1956, aged eighty-four. He had had a long innings, but not the great one forecast for him when he first went out to bat. He was cremated and his ashes taken not to the *Mercury* and the rose gardens, nor to any family resting place, but to Repton, there to be buried in the shadow of the parish church, with its slim elegant spire, and a few yards from a small gate in the boundary of the school where he may have known the only true happiness in his long and varied career. Always one of the most prestigious schools of its kind in the country, it is now co-educational, progressive and rich in the variety of opportunities it creates for its many students. It is marked throughout with his name on lists of its greatest achievers.

The departure of C.B. Fry and Sybil Hoare from the *Mercury* in 1950 was the end of an era. Many changes had to be made, beginning with the items of routine that owed more to the whims of the departing management than to established naval practice. One such whim was that of letting the movable feast of Easter define the school terms in a way totally at odds with those that generally prevailed. In its years as a charitable institution and for a few years after it became fee-paying there were only two terms. Nobody went home for an Easter break. In the mid-1920s it was changed to three, but, until the start of the Second World War, everyone, devout or otherwise, had to be on board for Easter weekend itself. An end was made to the stranger aspects of Saturday morning inspections, less emphasis was placed on the religious life, and the routine on the dormitory ship was overhauled. The tradition of singing an evening hymn was retained, however, and a lonely walker on Satchell Lane would hear, in the late evening, the bugle calls and the ethereal sound of a choir of 150 voices coming up from the darkened river. A duty officer could still order 'Abandon Ship!' sending boys rushing for the cutters, but as a necessary part of their training and not merely to impress the people in charge.

The new Captain Superintendent was a naval officer, Commander Matthew Bradby, MBE. Though the routine he ordained was less harsh and without the idiosyncrasies that had characterised the Fry era – bare feet and cropped heads were things of the past – the expectations were the same: hard work and disciplined effort. The curriculum was widened and schoolmasters were employed whose duties were confined to the classroom. Under the old regime they had had to wear uniform and were expected to supervise boys in a wide range of activities; now there were specialist teachers of literature, science, history, geography, languages – all the normal subjects of good secondary schooling – who wore their own clothes and were not expected to double as parade-ground disciplinarians.

Bradby was succeeded by Commander R.F. Hoyle in 1960, by which time the *Mercury* was in effect a residential grammar school, organised very much on the lines of the independent boarding schools, the best of which are regarded by many as being among the treasures of the British educational system. The nautical ingredient in the timetable was reduced to 25 per cent, and the end product was a young man who could think and perform over a wide range of subjects, and whose expectations were widened proportionately.

In 1968 the school was closed. The Royal and Merchant Navies, their fleets decreasing with the decline of empire, were seeking fewer and fewer recruits, and in any case the cost of running it had overtaken the available income. Admiral of the Fleet the Earl Mountbatten of Burma, president of the board of governors in the final years, attended the closing ceremonies. The boys were dispersed, mostly to the remaining grammar schools and to nautical colleges. Some went to HMS *Britannia*, the officer-training establishment at Dartmouth, others to HMS *Conway*, the officer cadet ship on the Mersey, the elite ship of its kind along with HMS *Worcester*, near Greenwich.

Over the next few years the deserted site at Hamble was cleared to make way for suburban houses. Nothing was saved. The clocktower, for which Beatie had dug the foundations, was supposed to have been spared, but one morning it was found in ruins, having been bulldozed in the night. The little chapel built by Charles Hoare was destroyed by fire in 1952 and a new one built, but this too was swept away. The destruction of the theatre, of Beatie's Building, was undoubtedly a prime piece of vandalism. An architectural gem, it had unmistakably Teutonic lines that would have looked good in a clearing in a Bavarian forest, but so beautifully achieved that they were far from incongruous in an English setting. Inside, it was a place of simple elegance, from the white balustrade that separated orchestra from auditorium, to the curve of the balcony. Schultz-Curtis, a German concert agent, loved this theatre and used to say that for sheer beauty of sound and acoustical purity he would sooner bring his artists there than to any other theatre in the land. Paradoxically, it became a haven for the boys who retreated into it as a place where they could be free of the tyranny of the woman whose ideas and drive brought it into being.

It was thus a hallowed place, having had added to design and utility an intrinsic worth that would not feature in an estate agent's accounts. The dancing, the plays and – most of all – the great music that had been performed within its mellow walls had given it that precious intangible, a soul. To destroy the quiet glory, the simple splendour, of the temple that housed that soul must remain in the minds of those who loved it as a piece of cold and unforgivable barbarism. There remains also the dismay that nothing was done to preserve a building that could have enriched the cultural and intellectual life of Hamble and the surrounding country. Instead, its bricks and mortar became the foundations of a car park.

The dormitory ship on the river, HMS *Gannet*, was towed away to Gosport in 1970 where a group of men who had trained on board made a brave try at restoring her. It was to prove too much for them, but their efforts served to keep her out of the hands of the breakers. She went at last to Chatham Historic Dockyard to be restored as an 'up screw, down funnel' sloop of the 1870s, the only one of its kind in existence. In her completed state she will be a memorial to the people who built her, to the men who sailed in her, to the thousands of boys who trained on board and to the woman who was in command for thirty-two of her fifty-four years on the Hamble.

The only other relics of the *Mercury* are the ship models collected by Charles Hoare and displayed in the National Maritime Museum, such as the royal yacht of 1685 and HMS *Tartar*, twenty guns, built in 1734, a tiny craft with every detail lovingly created by its maker, from the eponymous figure gripping the stem between his bare knees, to the carvings on the elaborate seven-windowed stern.

If little of the physical *Mercury* remains, the spirit of the school is alive for a time in the people who lived, taught and were taught there. A few leave words and works that will endure after their deaths. Peter Whitlock is an example of the pupil who went on to great things partly because of, and partly in spite of, his experiences. Vastly intelligent, highly trained, but poorly educated – the *Mercury* under Mrs Fry made few of the educational demands of the grammar school he might have attended – he entered the Royal Navy in 1940 as a rating and rose through the ranks to become a Lieutenant-Commander. Along the way he made himself a world authority on warships under sail, was appointed captain of HMS *Victory*, Nelson's flagship, and restored her to her condition at the time of the Battle of Trafalgar in 1805. He was a marine archaeologist, adviser to the team recovering the wreck of Henry VIII's *Mary Rose* and consultant to many others working on ancient wrecks. As a speaker he was without peer on his chosen subjects. He died in 1989 at the time when the victories of Nelson, his great hero, were being celebrated.

A deep impression was made on the world of music by Eric McGavin who left the ship to join Boosey & Hawkes of London, the music publishers and makers of musical instruments. A brilliant clarinettist, he travelled the country lecturing on his chosen instrument and fostering the growth of music in schools that led to the great youth orchestras of today. He himself founded the British Youth Wind Orchestra. He was made an honorary member of the Royal Academy of Music in recognition of his unique contribution to music in education. He died in 1970.

Of the thousands of men who began their careers on the *Mercury* many went on to hold high office in the Royal Navy, the Royal Marines and the Merchant Navy. Most of those of the post-Fry era, better equipped educationally, found work ashore and their achievements would have impressed Mrs Fry – who was not easily impressed. The passage of time will diminish their numbers, and the association they joined – which was strong at the beginning of the twenty-first century – will fade away, as must all such associations of men and women who meet out of nostalgia for the place, the institution or the person – no longer in existence – that brought them together. While they live their special aura derives from having been touched by history when they spent formative years on board the *Mercury*, the pre-sea school that was held together for sixty-one of its eighty-three years by a most remarkable woman.

'Freedom is messy', wrote Katharine Whitehorne in one of her columns in the London *Observer*, and this is most true when one has no clear idea of what one is striving to be free of and even less idea of what to do with the freedom gained. The fiery, impulsive girl who devastated her family, the devoted lover and the tyrant of the *Mercury*, probably acted out of no more than a gut reaction to the constraints of her time and her condition as a pawn in the machinations of her social class. In the pantheon of women who fought the same constraints there is no mention of her. At the pre-sea school of which she was the effective commander she did little for the true education of men, let alone of women, as her daughters might have testified. She seemed to have no feminist or political agenda. The struggles of the Suffragettes passed her by, her views only to be guessed at by the company she kept. She could not rank with the women adventurers of the nineteenth century who plunged into jungles, climbed mountains and crossed deserts. Three were born in the same decade as she was, two of them in the same year: Margaret Fountain two months before her and Mary Kingsley four months after. The third, Gertrude Bell, was born in 1868 and all three ranged the world while Beatie was tied to a ship that was going nowhere, the longest journey she could look back on being a chaperoned visit to Rome. On her eightieth birthday in 1942 she appeared briefly in jodhpurs, as if to say she wanted to be one with them.

Yet freedom was what Beatie – Beatrice Holme Fry – was about. It was the central paradox of her marriage to C.B. Fry that they both found a measure of freedom in it, one to amuse himself and, happily, many others for most of his remaining years, the other to take up a work of worth in an area which, without that marriage, was closed to her. It was the central irony that the partner whose free choice was a life of duty and discipline, the very things her husband extolled as long as they did not include himself, may have ended up the freer and, perhaps, the greater person.

Notes

MHNC: Margaret Hoare Newspaper Collection

Preface

1. John Arlott, in *Hampshire Magazine*, August 1971, p. 27.
2. J.B. Priestley, *The English*, 1973, p. 236.

Chapter 1

1. Author's papers

Chapter 2

1. Denzil Batchelor, *C.B. Fry*, 1951, p. 8.
2. *Ibid.*
3. MHNC.
4. *Hants Independent Weekly*, 23 May 1908.
5. MHNC.

Chapter 3

1. Bathurst, *A History of the VWH Country*, 1936, p. 152.
2. *Ibid.*, p. 153
3. MHNC.
4. *Ibid.*
5. K. Potter interviewed by the author in the early 1980s.

6. MHNC.
7. *Ibid.*
8. *Ibid.*
9. *Ibid.*
10. *Gloucester Chronicle*, 21 March 1885.
11. Charles Scott, Affidavit in PRO, J.4/2685/1486, 1885.
12. Beatrice Holme Sumner, Affidavit in PRO, J4/2685/1419, 1885.
13. *Ibid.*
14. *Ibid.*
15. Fitzhardinge Kingscote, Affidavit in PRO, J4/2416/2984001428, 1884.
16. James Kennelly, Affidavit in PRO, J4/2416/2983, May 1884.
17. Fitzhardinge Kingscote, Affidavit in PRO, 1884.
18. Alfred Inderwick, Affidavit in PRO, J4/2686/1575, 1885.
19. Fitzhardinge Kingscote, Affidavit in PRO, 1884.

Chapter 4

1. MHNC.
2. Alfred Inderwick, Affidavit in PRO, 1885.

3. Charles Hoare, Affidavit in PRO, J4/2419/3728, 1884.
4. Bathurst, *VWH Country*, p. 164.
5. *Ibid.*, p. 162.
6. *Ibid.*, p. 160.
7. *Ibid.*, p. 162.
8. MHNC.
9. Bathurst, *VWH Country*, p. 165.
10. Fitzhardinge Kingscote, Affidavit in PRO, 1884.
11. James Kennelly, Affidavit in PRO, 1885.
12. Robert Blott, Affidavit in PRO. J4/2685/1494, 1884.
13. Hoare, Affidavit in PRO, 1884.
14. *Wilts and Gloucestershire Standard*.
15. *Ibid.*
16. Law Reports, 17 March 1885, Court of Chancery.

Chapter 5

1. *The Times*, 18 March 1885.
2. Beatrice Holme Sumner, Affidavit in PRO, 1885.
3. *Ibid.*
4. Rt Hon. The Marchioness of Cholmondeley, Affidavit in PRO, J4/2686/1503, 1885.
5. Alfred Inderwick, Affidavit in PRO, J4/2416/2990, 20 May 1884.
6. Nigel Kingscote, Affidavit in PRO, J4/2416/2990, 1885.
7. A.R. Huitt, Affidavit in PRO, J4/2685/1420, 1885.
8. For accounts of the case, see *The Times*, 18 and 19 March 1885; *Gloucestershire Chronicle*, 21 March 1885; *The People*, 22 March 1885; *Reynolds Newspaper*, 22 March 1885; *News of the World*, 22 March 1885.
9. *Sumner v. Kingscote* (1885) 1 TLR 351.
10. *Truth*, 26 March 1885.
11. *Vanity Fair*, 21 March 1885, p. 167.

Chapter 6

1. *Wilts and Gloucestershire Standard*, 2 May 1885.
2. J. Moore of Bulmer, Yorkshire, in letters to the author.
3. MHNC.
4. *Mercury* log.
5. Colin Ridge.
6. MHNC.
7. Bathurst papers.
8. Bathurst, papers, p. 182.
9. *Ibid.*, p. 82.
10. *Ibid.*, p. 183.

Chapter 7

1. Mercury Old Boys' Association (MOBA) collection of papers.
2. Gibraltar Port Records, researched by K. Travis, MOBA.
3. Rebecca Livingston of the National Archives, Washington DC, USA.
4. K. Travis.
5. John Munday, Keeper, Department of Antiquities, National Maritime Museum.
6. Lord Rosebery, quoted in

J.B. Priestley, *The English*, p. 72.

7. Plaque preserved in St Andrew's, Hamble parish church, the south courtyard.

8. Canto IV, stanza CXL.

Chapter 8

1. Sir George Schuster, in a letter to the author.
2. MOBA papers: staff register.
3. L.G. Charles, in letters to the author.
4. *Southern Daily Echo*, 8 September 1956.
5. *Mercury Magazine*, 1907–8.
6. *Ibid.*

Chapter 9

1. A.R. Cooper, in *The Captain* (ed. C.B. Fry), May 1909.
2. Lytton Strachey, *Eminent Victorians*, 1918.
3. Adria Hoare, daughter-in-law of Charles Hoare, from an interview with the author.
4. J. Moore: original research on behalf of the author.
5. MOBA Collection.
6. Staff log, TS *Mercury*.

Chapter 10

1. E. Walker, in letters to the author.
2. MOBA Collection.
3. Henry Gardner, *Autobiography*, 1979.
4. Colin Ridge, in letters to the author.

5. E.P. Hunter, in letters to the author.
6. A.L.E. Hoskyns-Abrahall, interviewed by the author.
7. *Mercury Magazine*, December 1926.
8. *Ibid.*
9. *Ibid.*
10. *Mercury Magazine*, December 1928.
11. *Mercury Magazine*, 1931.
12. *Ibid.*
13. *Ibid.*
14. *Ibid.*
15. *Ibid.*
16. *Mercury Magazine*, 1921.
17. *Mercury Magazine*, 1926.
18. Captain R.E. Hutchins, RN, in interview and in letters to the author.
19. Mrs Casimir, in letters to the author.

Chapter 11

1. Royal Archives, Windsor.
2. Admiral of the Fleet the Rt Hon. the Earl Mountbatten of Burma, in a letter to the author.
3. National Maritime Museum: a collection of letters about the Hoare Collection of ship models.
4. E. Walker, in letters to the author.
5. Lieutenant W. Mobsby, RN, in letters to the author.
6. E.W. Swanton, *Sort of a Cricketing Person*, p. 188.
7. Stephen Fry, in an interview with the author.

8. *The Daily Echo*, Southampton, 14 March 1998 and letters exchanged by the author and Michael Ware, Curator, the National Motor Museum, Beaulieu.

9. National Maritime Museum, newspaper archives, 23 February 1934.

10. P. Toghill, R. Morris and J. Waite, 'C.B. Fry: Thwarted Genius?', *Journal of Medical Biography*, vol. 7, 1999.

11. See C.B. Fry, *Life Worth Living*, Eyre and Spottiswoode, 1939.

12. Neville Cardus, *Autobiography*, p. 150.

Chapter 12

1. *Southern Daily Echo*, 23 April 1946.

2. *Mercury Magazine*, 1927.

Epilogue

1. Samuel Johnson, *Lives of the Poets*.

2. Sir Maurice Bowra, *Memories*, p. 32.

3. Birkenhead, *The Life of F.E. Smith*, p. 32.

Bibliography

Batchelor, Denzil, *C.B. Fry* (in the series 'Cricketing Lives'), London, 1951

Bathurst, the 7th Earl, *A History of the VWH Country*, London, 1936

Birkenhead, the 2nd Earl, *F.E.: The Life of F.E. Smith, First Earl of Birkenhead*, London, 1959

Bowra, Sir Maurice, *Memories*, London, 1966

Cardus, Sir Neville, *Autobiography*, London, 1961

Fry, C.B., *Life Worth Living*, London, 1939

Gardner, Henry, unpublished MS, 'Autobiography', in the National Maritime Museum, Greenwich, London

Kingscote Papers, unpublished collection of papers, property of Miss K. Potter

Margaret Hoare Collection, unpublished collection of newspaper cuttings, property of Michael Hoare

Mercury Old Boys' Association Papers, unpublished collection of papers, property of MOBA

Priestley, J.B., *The English*, 1973

Strachey, Lytton, *Eminent Victorians*, London, Chatto & Windus, 1974

Swanton, E.W., *Sort of a Cricketing Person*, London, 1972

Toghill P., Morris R. and Waite, J.: 'C.B. Fry: Thwarted Genius?' *Journal of Medical Biography*, vol. 7, 1999

Index